5

THE POLITICS OF THE EN

THE POLITICS OF
THE ENVIRONMENT

STEPHEN C YOUNG

First published 1993 by
Baseline Book Company
PO Box 34
Chorlton
Manchester M21 1LL

British Library Cataloguing in Publication Data

ISBN 1 897626 04 5

Cover design   Ian Price
Cover illustration   Min Cooper
Typesetting   Kathryn Holliday
Printed and bound by Nuffield Press, Oxford

CONTENTS

FIGURES AND TABLES

FIGURES

TABLES

ACKNOWLEDGEMENTS

It is customary in green circles to say a bit about where you are coming from. On reflection I can see now that much of my life has led towards this book. It is inevitable, when it ranges so widely, that I owe much to people I have met outside the academic world. Along the way there has been the wisdom of the crofter, the resourcefulness of the hill farmer, and the perspectives of those who have had time to stand back from making things happen in local government to wonder about how services might be provided in more flexible, less heavy-handed, less bureaucratic ways. I have also learnt much from my involvement with committees and voluntary organisations in the environmental and wildlife fields. I am particularly grateful for all I have absorbed from colleagues on the Council of the Town and Country Planning Association.

Looking back I can see it is not just the people either. I have been learning about a sense of wonder at the natural world since my childhood: from the newts in the pond near where I lived then, right through exploring wild places with Nin, Simon and David, and with Anne; to the roosting sparrowhawk that sits in the tree outside my office as I write.

I lived for 20 years high in the Pennines in the West Riding of Yorkshire, and learnt much from its landscape, as well as from its people. The experience of trying to cope with the demands of running an organic smallholding – part of which turned out to be a Site of Special Scientific Interest – gave me a whole new perspective on how the natural world fits together, and how people relate to it. There is time to think while you hand-milk a cow. Like many others there, I watched the decline of local industry; the loss of local control over economic decisions; the attempts at regeneration via services, tourism and not-for-profit experiments; and wondered about *how* small could be beautiful.

In the early 1990s I have much appreciated the stimulating company of academic colleagues: Michael Waller, Dick Richardson, Andy Dobson, Neil Carter, Brian Doherty, and Graham Smith among the many others I mention. I must also include Chris Wood and Chris Bannister and their colleagues in the Planning and Landscape Department at Manchester University where I have spent so much of my teaching time. I have also benefited from the clash of opinions amongst the students doing my

Green Politics course in the Department of Government at Manchester. Despite all this, I must remain responsible for what follows.

The fact that this book has happened is due to the support of my publisher Ian Holliday, and the typing skills of Shahnaz Holder and Joanne Crolla-Parkhouse. For their contributions I am most grateful. But most of all I am indebted to Anne; not just for her love and patience, but for her company, her laughter and her realism during the many expeditions that have contributed to what follows.

A book like this has to be dedicated to future generations: to the quality of life of today's school children when they are pensioners, and to the hope that there will still be remote and wild places for them to enjoy.

Stephen C Young
September 1993

ABBREVIATIONS

bvk	Billion vehicle kilometres
CC	Countryside Commission
CFC	Chlorofluorocarbon
CPRE	Council for the Protection of Rural England
CSD	UN Commission on Sustainable Development
CSR	Corporate social responsibility
DoE	Department of the Environment
DTI	Department of Trade and Industry
DTp	Department of Transport
EIA	Environmental Impact Assessment
EPA	Environmental Protection Act 1990
ES	Environmental Statement
ESA	Environmentally Sensitive Area
FoE	Friends of the Earth
GNP	Gross National Product
HMIP	Her Majesty's Inspectorate of Pollution
IPC	Integrated pollution control
IWC	International Whaling Commission
LETS	Local exchange trading system
MAFF	Ministry of Agriculture, Fisheries and Food
NASA	National Aeronautics and Space Administration
NCC	Nature Conservancy Council
NGO	Non-governmental organisation
NFU	National Farmers' Union
NRA	National Rivers Authority
NSM	New social movement
OECD	Organisation for Economic Cooperation and Development
OFFER	Office of Electricity Regulation
QGA	Quasi-governmental agency
RSNC	Royal Society for Nature Conservation
RSPB	Royal Society for the Protection of Birds
TCPA	Town and Country Planning Association
TFO	Third-force organisation
WDA	Waste Disposal Authority
WRA	Waste Regulation Authority
WWF	World Wide Fund for Nature

INTRODUCTION

The environment is a huge multi-dimensional issue going way beyond attempts to conserve the countryside. This book outlines the nature and variety of the environmental problems that face contemporary governments and sets them in their economic, social and political contexts. It focuses mainly on Britain, but ranges widely in drawing together ideas that are dispersed across a huge literature. It covers everything from local initiatives to action at the international level. Its main aim is to condense the ideas and government responses into a succinct and readable account without getting lost in jargon.

THE EXTENT OF THE CHALLENGE

A further aim of this book is to argue the need for individuals and governments at all levels to take the environment more seriously than is currently the case. Stewart and Hams argue that 'Human economic activity is taking resources faster than the planet can replenish them and producing wastes faster than the planet can absorb them. If this continues it will destroy the planet's ability to support human life'.[1] The extent of the environmental challenge could not be put more clearly.

This book is concerned both to analyse the nature of the environmental crisis and to outline ways in which it can be tackled. It therefore explains the initial changes of tack that are needed to correct the current situation, whilst recognising that the process of change will inevitably be very drawn out. It is neither a tale of woe, nor a utopian tract. It sets out the debates about the options from the perspective of both reforming governments and radical greens so readers can draw their own conclusions about where they stand.

STRUCTURE OF ARGUMENT

Chapter 1 sets out the range of issues, from the neighbourhood to the atmosphere, that together constitute the environmental crisis. Chapter 2 looks at the scope of protest by environmental groups, and their impact. Chapter 3 focuses on the successes and failures of green parties around the world.

Chapter 4 examines international dimensions, concentrating on the aftermath of the Rio Summit and the role of the European Commission. Chapter 5 analyses environmental policies in Britain, looking especially at what has happened since 1988 when Margaret Thatcher suddenly started to make speeches about the environment.

Chapter 6 moves on to examine how far policies aimed at companies and individuals have had an impact. Chapter 7 compares Britain's record with those of other countries. Chapter 8 discusses challenges facing governments as they try to adopt new policies.

Chapter 9 subjects the preceding chapters to a green critique. The aim here is to contrast the emerging conventional wisdom with the perspective of radical greens. The Conclusion draws together some of the main themes and sets out ways in which the reader can work out where he or she stands on environmental issues.

NOTE

1 J Stewart and T Hams, *Local Government for Sustainable Development* (Local Government Management Board, Luton, 1992), p.7.

1 THE ENVIRONMENTAL CRISIS

The first problem with analysing the politics of the environment is understanding the scope of what 'environment' covers. The initial aim of this chapter is to set out the range and breadth of what analysts refer to when using phrases like 'environmental problems' or 'environmental issues'. During the 1980s the environment was like a basket which grew bigger and bigger as more and more was thrown into it.

ANALYTICAL APPROACH

The approach taken here is to look at the environment from both the bottom up and the top down. This chapter starts from the point of view of an individual's daily life in a developed industrial society like Britain. But this is only one side of the coin because what we do in Britain has international consequences contributing to wider problems, as when we add to sea pollution levels.

There are also a number of environmental problems which are in an altogether different league. An example is the growth of population which has substantial implications for demands placed on resources. Such issues have a more radical effect on the planet itself. So apart from taking a bottom-up perspective, this chapter also explores truly global issues. It unravels the scope and range of environmental issues by looking at them from the top down, from the planet's perspective.

THE ENVIRONMENT FROM THE INDIVIDUAL'S PERSPECTIVE

People experience many problems in their local environment. Whether they live in cities, towns or the countryside, they are confronted, almost on a daily basis, by things like foul air, litter, noise, derelict waste land, pollution and pesticides. Most upsetting of all is the loss of a favourite place, often near to home, when a new road, superstore or other development is built.

The way we experience environmental problems makes it seem as if they are isolated from each other. We see traffic congestion from a living room window, or foaming polluted river water from a bus. Such incidents appear to be problems *out there* that can be isolated and treated. But analysis shows a much greater complexity. Environmental problems are linked to each other. They have knock-on effects. The first point to establish is that what appear to be little local difficulties are the visible parts of much more complicated sets of inter-related problems. What we see are the tips of icebergs.

This can be illustrated by means of a dartboard approach to defining the range and breadth of environmental issues. At the centre of the dartboard in Figure 1.1 there are the visible environmental problems which can be seen where people live. Moving outwards we encounter another set of problems created by the immediately visible mess. These are the wider dimensions of the local problems at the centre. Geographically they are situated in the surrounding sub-region or within the same country. Moving outwards again, the third ring represents the transnational or even global problems that result from the initial local problems.

Figure 1.1 Dartboard approach to defining the range and breadth of environmental problems

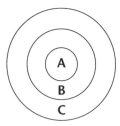

A = Local and visible problems
B = Problems created by the local ones, situated in the surrounding sub-region or within the same country
C = Transnational and global problems

Several problems arise with water that are local and visible. Streams, rivers and stretches of coast get polluted; tap water can be dirty; and supplies can be inadequate. Further afield, in the second circle, polluted rivers kill wildlife, make swimmers and canoeists ill, and create unpleasant smells, thereby undermining the recreational benefits of the area. The same happens with polluted beaches. Unfit drinking water causes ill health. Inadequate supplies of water can limit building options in areas judged to be suitable for development. In the outside circle on the diagram, there are consequences when polluted rivers like the Mersey and the Rhine enter the sea; when sewage sludge is dumped in the North Sea and other oceans; or when the effects of coastal pollution incidents are spread more widely. The health of fish stocks may be affected. Shell fish in particular may become unfit for human consumption. Radioactivity may seep into the Irish Sea. The breeding success of sea birds, seals and other creatures is also undermined by diminished or unhealthy food sources in polluted areas. The cumulative effects of different water pollution incidents thus cause international problems far from their point of origin.

Starting at the centre of the dartboard again, individuals see rubbish locally in terms of their own dustbin, the fly-tipping of old cars and furniture, and perhaps the disposal of waste at work. Moving outwards on the diagram, the main consequence of waste disposal is its collection and management. Landfill sites take 90 per cent of Britain's waste, much of it coming from agricultural, commercial and industrial sources. This all creates a big need for suitable sites. They have to be chosen carefully to avoid such problems as liquid leaching out and damaging water supplies and surrounding land. Incinerators – of hospital waste for example – lead to complaints of particles falling to earth on washing in nearby gardens. Another unseen aspect of waste at the sub-regional level is the continuing need to clear up the consequences of past actions. There are sites where land has been polluted by the dumping of chemicals; and where development has taken place on former waste tips where there is the threat of methane gas building up. At the international level, in the outer ring, toxic waste substances are a hazard. Dangerous chemicals and radioactive materials find their way into water courses and into the seas where they are not absorbed.

Several environmental problems arise with a roads-based transport policy. Starting at the centre of the dartboard, individuals can see traffic congestion, lengthening rush hours, and the way in which cars are allowed to dominate cities to the detriment of children in push-chairs, pedestrians, bus users and cyclists. Where new roads take land they often damage areas of countryside and sites of value to wildlife. Moving outwards on the diagram, there are the less evident problems. People living near major road arteries are affected by noise, toxic lead fumes, and higher rates of asthma from the polluted air.

The roads programme spreads development more widely and generates more traffic. It also creates a demand for aggregates. As a result of opposition to further quarrying in national parks and the Thames Valley, sites are being developed further afield. The 1990s approach is the concept of the super-quarry. This involves carving huge amounts of stone out of Scottish mountains and taking them to sites where roads are being built. At the transnational level, increases in road traffic add to the acid rain problem, worsen the greenhouse effect, and further deplete oil reserves.

Space precludes a detailed discussion of other issues in terms of the dartboard approach. But it can be applied to air pollution, energy, agriculture, food and forestry, and other environmental issues. Starting from the perspective of where people live, it is possible to work out the wider, less visible problems which occur further afield.

GLOBAL ENVIRONMENTAL ISSUES

Having looked at the environment from the bottom-up viewpoint of the individual in a developed industrial democracy, the focus now shifts to the other extreme. This section explores the scope and range of environmental issues from the top down, from the perspective of the planet. This is a slightly artificial divide as the two overlap. The individual's use of a car in Britain, for example, is part of one country's contribution to the problem of global warming. But this approach does highlight the next stage in the argument: the impact of human activity on the *health of the planet itself*. More specifically, we should talk of the planet and the surrounding atmosphere, which is often referred to as the biosphere.

There are a number of problems here. What follows is a brief summary of the issues.[1] They have many dimensions and are interconnected in all sorts of ways. The pattern of cause and effect is complex. For presentational purposes they are divided into two groups. First, there are obviously and explicitly environmental problems which have a direct impact on the health of the planet. Then there are broader and more complex problems which have environmental consequences, and thus an indirect effect on the planet. The two groups are analysed in separate sections.

EXPLICITLY ENVIRONMENTAL PROBLEMS

The first direct environmental problem is **pollution of the earth itself**. Pesticides and herbicides banned in the North are used in third-world countries. Toxic waste is exported there. Apart from the side effects on people, this leads to pollution of the land, and causes chemicals to seep into water courses. Rivers affect oceans, adding to the waste that is dumped there. This further interferes with the food chain. The effects are concentrated when there are major disasters like the 1984 chemical explosion at Bhopal in India which killed 2500 and affected 300 000 others; or the 1989 *Exxon Valdese* Alaskan oil-spill. The other form of pollution to note here is acid rain in northern Europe, North America and parts of India and China. It affects not just forests and lakes, but rivers, seas, crops and buildings. In the background there is the threat of a nuclear accident from a military or terrorist source, as well as from another incident like Chernobyl.

Moving further away from the planet to about 12 to 30 miles above the earth, the problem of **the ozone layer** threatens the whole biosphere. The ozone layer protects all forms of life on earth from the harmful effects of the sun's ultra-violet rays. It is being depleted. Holes have actually emerged over the Arctic, and between Australia and Antarctica. In 1993, a National Aeronautics and Space Administration (NASA) report identified a hole in the ozone layer over Europe, and unprecedented thinning over Britain. Damage to the ozone layer leads to cataracts and cancers in humans. The latter have become much more common in Australia since about 1970. Depletion also threatens plant growth in lakes and oceans, and thus the food-chain.

Thirdly, there is **the greenhouse effect**. This is the artificial warming of the atmosphere around the earth. It is caused by accumulation of man-made gases. Heat from the sun that is reflected from the earth is trapped and cannot escape into space. As a result, the biosphere's self-regulating system cannot function properly and the earth warms up. This has set in chain processes of global warming and climate change. These lead to rising sea levels, drought, and storms which cause floods and crop failures. The 1990 Intergovernmental Panel on Climate Change forecast a rise of 1°C every 30 years, on top of the 0.6°C rise which has been registered during the past century. By contrast, a drop of 4°C would spark off a full ice age. A 3°C temperature rise by the end of the next century is therefore serious, though perhaps not as immediately serious as depletion of the ozone layer.

What stands out here is the importance of man-made gases as the main cause of significant problems: acid rain, ozone depletion, and the greenhouse effect. Acid rain is caused by the interaction of gases emitted from vehicle exhausts, and from the burning of coal and oil, especially in power stations. The main cause of ozone depletion is chlorofluorocarbons (CFCs) used in aerosols, refrigerators, air conditioners, and foam blowing for things like hamburger cartons, car seats, polystyrene, and insulation materials. CFCs also account for about one-fifth of the gases causing the greenhouse effect.

The other two main gases here are methane and carbon dioxide. Both occur naturally. Carbon dioxide in particular plays an important part in filtering the sun's rays and in stabilising the global climate system. But economic activity has added to the volume of these two gases in the atmosphere and altered the balance of the biosphere's self-regulating system. Methane accounts for about one-sixth of the greenhouse effect. The increase here is caused by rice paddies, livestock digestion, landfill sites and the burning of industrial wastes. Carbon dioxide emissions are more significant, accounting for about half of all greenhouse gases. Three-quarters of these emissions come from the burning of coal, oil and natural gases for electricity and from vehicles. Britain's power stations and motorway building programmes fit in here. The other quarter comes from the burning of tropical rain forests. This destruction is the fourth of the international environmental problems with a direct impact on the biosphere.

Tropical rain forests used to cover about 14 per cent of the land around the equator. About half of them have been destroyed, and at current rates virtually all will have disappeared by 2020. Apart from the link to the greenhouse effect, and the impact on local tribes, these forests are important in other ways. First, leaves absorb carbon dioxide and release oxygen during the process of photosynthesis. Removing excess carbon dioxide helps to regulate the greenhouse effect. Second, rain forests help stabilise global weather patterns, particularly in connection with North American farming areas. Third, they are the most species-rich habitats on earth, containing more than half of the 30 million species on the planet. More than a quarter of all medicines contain compounds drawn from plants that can only be found in tropical rain forests.

Destruction of rain forests has important implications for the last of the five international environmental problems. This is **biodiversity**

and the extinction of species. Apart from habitat destruction in all parts of the world, other causes are the use of chemicals in agriculture, over-exploitation, and international trade in pets. Examples of these processes in the British case are loss of hedgerows, use of pesticides, over-fishing at sea, and imports of tropical birds as pets.

Reducing the variety of plant and animal species on earth will have several effects. First, there are implications for feeding the world's growing population. Genetic variety is needed to develop new plants and to strengthen strains that are becoming more susceptible to disease. Local varieties of vegetables have been lost in Britain in the drive towards standardisation and high yields. A similar story can be told about strains of rice – and species of pigs and cattle. Next, decline in biodiversity will affect the development of biotechnology, medicines and other products. We simply do not know which species will have significance for our grandchildren. Finally, the loss of species has indefinable consequences for evolution as a whole. Rees likens the loss of species to pulling threads from a tapestry.[2] To start with it looks the same. Then suddenly the whole thing falls apart. With biodiversity, we do not understand the dimensions of what we are tampering with.

BROAD INTERNATIONAL PROBLEMS WITH ENVIRONMENTAL IMPACTS ON THE BIOSPHERE

Here, the first problem is rapid increase in **global population levels**. It took until 1830 to reach the first billion people on earth, and another century to reach the second. There were 4 billion people by 1974, and 5.3 billion by 1990. Levels are expected to top 6 billion by 2000, to reach 8 billion by 2025 and 10 billion by 2050. Almost all of this population growth is in third-world countries, where it intensifies the next problem.

The **shortage of food and clean drinking water** in the third world has a number of dimensions. These include problems concerning food distribution, malnutrition, polluted drinking water, and in many places the threat of persistent famine. Widespread shortages coexist with exports of grain to help produce meat in developed countries. In rich countries, such as EC member states, surpluses are stored or destroyed. As with environmental problems at the local level in developed industrial societies, these environmental problems also have major social dimensions.

The next problem is **third-world poverty**. In rural areas survival depends on cultivating poor, marginal land, or on clearing forests for fuel and pasture. Over-cultivation and over-grazing create conditions for soil erosion. The American dust bowl experience of the 1930s is repeated: grasslands become desert, and people move to other areas where the cycle starts again and desertification spreads further. In some parts of the world, eroded top soil ends up in rivers, where it aggravates flooding. Hunger and poverty drive people to cities in search of food and work. All too often the result is further poverty in the environmentally-degraded conditions of the shanty town.

During the 1980s, increasing numbers of those trying to scratch a living on the edge of a desert or city set off on longer journeys, thereby creating the fourth big problem, **environmental refugees**. Escaping from flood, drought, desertification and poverty, people move much further than the nearest city, crossing frontiers to start new lives. In 1978 there were about 5 million political refugees. In 1992, it was estimated that there were about 25 million environmental refugees or economic migrants. The American Woods Hole Institute estimates that 40 million Bangladeshis will be forced to move by 2050 because of a two-metre rise in the sea level. Population growth rates in the Indian sub-continent are amongst the world's highest. In such circumstances saturation point will be reached and people will be forced to move on a huge scale. In 1993 California had 1.3 million undocumented immigrants. In the nineteenth century there was space for dispossessed crofters and European refugees to start new lives in Australia or the USA. Now, as America reviews its attitudes and people speak of 'Fortress Europe', this threatens to become an increasingly significant problem, especially as population levels rise further.

The next problem is **third-world debt**. In the early 1970s much of the income from growing oil consumption was converted into loans to third-world countries. Their plans to repay the debt and accumulated interest were undermined by recession, falling commodity prices and increased interest rates. In addition, rich countries erected trade barriers, making it harder for third-world countries to earn income from exports. Third-world debt went up from $748 million in 1981 to $1319 million in 1988. Sub-Saharan debt more than doubled between 1982 and 1990. Consequently, third-world countries have turned increasingly to exploitation of their environmental assets, like minerals and fisheries, as a way of repaying debts. This has had severe environmental consequences. The way in which over-grazing and over-cultivation leads to desertification is described above. Other examples are clearing tropical rain forests to sell timber, and cattle ranching to supply the hamburger trade.

Finally, there is the problem of **the North/South divide**. The rich North is usually taken to mean the industrialised democracies, predominantly in North America and western Europe, that make up the Organisation for Economic Cooperation and Development (OECD). The South refers to the third-world countries of Africa, Asia and Latin America. The essence of the divide is generated by the North's monopoly of resources, including investment capital, technology and purchasing power in the international economy. The richest third consumes two-thirds of all resources. The OECD countries have about 16 per cent of the world's population. Their relatively successful economies lead to much higher energy consumption rates and standards of living, even in inner-city areas. It is often said that cats in the North eat more meat than do many people in the third world.

The divide makes it much more difficult to tackle environmental problems in the South. Third-world economies become trapped, orientated towards the need to repay debts to the North, rather than towards addressing issues associated with poverty. These include malnutrition, poor housing, low levels of education, lack of fresh water, inadequate sanitation, and so on. In addition, almost all current population growth is in the South. This adds to pressures on already limited resources to tackle what are huge problems.

The net effect of the divide is two-fold. First, it intensifies and extends the problems of famine, poverty, growing numbers of migrants, and debt outlined above. Second, the negative effects of these issues on the environment will continue. The increase in forecast world population levels is likely to extend pressures on the environment, and to lead to further damage. Meanwhile, the North's consumer-based, materialist life style is conveyed around the world via advertising, TV, and multi-national activity as a model for governments and individuals in the South to copy.

The South's perspective on these problems is based on three points. To begin with, third-world countries argue that as the North has been responsible for most of the problems, making all of the peoples of the world suffer, it should take a greater lead in tackling them, fostering technology transfer, and paying for programmes. OECD countries produce three-quarters of the world's industrial waste and four-fifths of its hazardous wastes. Second, the South wants help with the debt issue and with the scale of its problems. Only then can the two inter-related issues of development and environmental problems be tackled. Finally, the South argues that the North has no moral right to limit development in third-world countries as a means of addressing environmental problems. Northern governments appear to think that fast growth, industrialisation and development in the South would further deplete the ozone layer and worsen the greenhouse effect and other global problems. The South feels that the North protects standards of living in the North while denying improvements to the South.

THE ENVIRONMENTAL CRISIS

So far this chapter has summarised the complex set of inter-related environmental problems which has emerged at all levels from the neighbourhood to the biosphere. Only some are visible at the local level. The root cause of these problems has been humankind's attitude to the environment. To begin with, the environment has been – and still is – treated like a sink. Farmers and industrialists assume that they can allow their waste products to escape into the atmosphere or into water courses. They do not have to pay the cost of cleaning up. These are external costs paid by others which are not part of the cost of running a farm or factory. These are the 'externalities' that economists talk about.

In addition, the cumulative effects of human actions on the environment have been ignored. Although treatment of the environment as a sink has been witnessed since the Industrial Revolution in the North, it has a far longer history.[3] Other species use their environment to live and breed. But humans have exploited their environment regardless of the damage thereby caused.

This approach has two consequences for the environment itself. These are the two dimensions of the environmental crisis. First, there is **the health of the biosphere**. Put simply, we depend on the planet, but we are in danger of destroying its ability to support human and other forms of life. Rivers and oceans can clean themselves naturally if they have enough time. But they cannot deal with the quantities of pollution that are currently discharged. In addition, some chemicals are very long lasting. The cumulative effects of millions of human actions are, collectively, undermining the health of the biosphere. The seriousness of widespread habitat loss, the implications of the greenhouse effect for climate change, and the problems posed by population increases are not fully understood. The extent to which permanent damage has already been caused to the biosphere is not clear. Finally, no one knows whether there is a threshold to ozone depletion, beyond which things will rapidly worsen.

The second dimension to the environmental crisis is that **existing approaches to economic growth cannot be sustained**. This is the case first because natural resources are limited, and subject to greater future demand because of population forecasts. Second, there is the point that unrestrained economic growth will aggravate the other dimension to the environmental crisis. It will cause more and more damage to the environment. This will further endanger the health of the biosphere.

It was into the debate surrounding these issues that the Brundtland Report was launched in 1987.[4] It set out the concept of sustainable development as a means of tackling the environmental crisis.

EIGHT KEY DIMENSIONS OF SUSTAINABLE DEVELOPMENT

The Brundtland Report provides the much-quoted definition of sustainable development. Development needs to be sustainable 'to ensure that it meets the needs of the present without compromising the ability of future generations to meet their own needs'.[5] This definition is deceptively simple. It has been criticised for being too vague and generalised. Politicians confuse it with the idea of sustained economic growth. This ignores the environmental impact of such growth. The concept is explored here by breaking it into eight key ideas.[6]

● **Futurity** The starting point is the need to consider the impact of our economic activity on the ability of future generations to meet their needs. It is thus necessary to consider new developments against a much longer time-horizon than the 15 years or so that local authority plans apply at present, or the three or four years (often less) till the next election that politicians think in terms of. Wardens preparing management plans for nature reserves look far further into the future and provide a much better example. It takes an oak tree up to 400 years to mature. This is the time horizon they work towards.

- **Inter-generational equity** Future generations should have access to the same resource base as existing generations, which means managing the resource base effectively, and passing on constant or improving capital stock. The latter covers such things as physical assets, financial capital, institutions that protect the environment, and environmental assets like new forests.[7]
- **Intra-generational equity** One of Brundtland's main concerns was the need to tackle third-world poverty. Equity between existing generations is about meeting basic needs of food, shelter and work. It is thus about redistribution and approaches that discriminate in favour of the disadvantaged, both in the third world, and in the deprived inner-city communities of the rich North.
- **Participation** This is closely linked to intra-generational equity. The essence of the argument is that if there is to be positive discrimination in favour of poorer groups and minorities, then such groups have to be closely involved in defining their own needs. The way this is put into practice in different societies will vary. In developed industrial societies like Britain, it means moving beyond a situation in which patterns of economic development are determined primarily by business and other articulate groups. It means involving women, ethnic groups, the disabled, young people and other disadvantaged minorities in constructive dialogues with government agencies so that their needs can be met more effectively than is the case at present.
- **The need to consider environmental costs in decision-making processes** Throughout history decisions about investment projects have largely focused on economic costs and on whether schemes are financially viable. This links to the earlier point about regarding the environment as a sink for waste products, and ignoring externalities. Growing appreciation of the seriousness of environmental issues like the greenhouse effect and ozone depletion has led to a reassessment. There is now widespread agreement on the need to take environmental costs into account when making decisions. The difficulties involved in putting this into practice are discussed in Chapter 9.
- **Environmental capacities** This relates to the capacity of the planet to cope with human demands on it. The environment can absorb our wastes, but only so long as the rates at which they are deposited do not exceed certain thresholds. If these are breached, as with acid rain, for example, the planet can no longer provide resources of fish and timber, operate the carbon cycle, and maintain the natural world. It is thus necessary to assess what these thresholds are so that policies can be developed to ensure that environmental carrying capacities are not exceeded.

● **Economic growth that stresses quality, not quantity** Sustainable development is concerned to change the nature of economic activity to make it compatible with environmental needs. This involves economic activity that does not permanently damage the environment. In the energy field, redesigned buildings, insulation measures, and expansion of renewable sources could actually cut the demand for energy during a period of economic growth. This would then reduce the contribution of power stations to the greenhouse effect. Another important part of making economic activity compatible with sustainable development is promoting jobs that 'go with the grain' of the environment and help improve environmental conditions. This aspect is explored further in Chapter 8.

● **Compatability with local eco-systems** So often there is a delicate balance in nature which human intervention destroys, as with the planting of conifers in the Scottish flow country. It is however possible to promote wildlife with farming, and to set new industrial or housing schemes in the context of wildlife corridors. The aim is to cut out or minimise damage to local eco-systems, and to promote ecologically-sustainable development.

FEATURES OF THE ENVIRONMENTAL CRISIS

Several points stand out from this initial discussion. One is the sheer complexity of environmental issues. What appear to be isolated local problems are actually the visible parts of complex sets of inter-related problems. People complain that the environment as it is presented is too big, that the basket is too huge to handle. The reality is that it is a multi-dimensional issue. It covers every aspect of the relationship people have with their natural environment. This includes air, water and land. It is much more than just protecting the countryside.

The second point is that the environment is in part a social issue. Growing levels of traffic in cities have led to significant increases in incidences of asthma, particularly among children. This is the case in San Francisco, as it is in Germany and Britain. There are other ways in which local environments are degraded. What appears to be a narrow issue broadens out to be about people's housing and surroundings – in fact about the quality of local living conditions. The same is true in the third world.

Finally, action to tackle environmental problems is required at different levels of government. Starting from the bottom there is local government. One of the major points to emerge from the 1992 Rio Summit was consensus around the idea that most problems needed to be tackled at the local level, not the national. Moving up, and of particular importance in the British case, is the level of the quasi-governmental agency (QGA) which is autonomous from government (at least to some extent), but funded by it. Next, national governments have some problems to address. Investment in public transport is an example in the British case. Finally, there is the international level. Sometimes transnational problems – such as pollution of the Rhine – implicate several governments. Major problems like global warming and ozone depletion, however, call for worldwide cooperation.

In practice there is another level of activity. Many initiatives take place at the level of local communities in villages or urban neighbourhoods. Environmental improvement schemes and waste recycling projects often operate within a framework set out by the local authority.

Two of the recurring themes of this book arise from the point about the need for action at different levels. First, the community level of action relates to the theme of empowering people to tackle environmental problems. Second, the most significant levels of action are at the local and international levels. The nation state is not redundant, but it has a less important role to play, especially in countries like Germany, Switzerland and the USA which have federal governments.

NOTES

1 This section draws from A Rees, *The Pocket Green Book* (Zed Books, London, 1991); P Ekins *et al.*, *Wealth Beyond Measure* (Gaia, London, 1992); S Yearley, *The Green Case* (Harper Collins, London, 1991); A Blowers (ed), *Planning for a Sustainable Environment* (Earthscan, London, 1993), ch.1; Department of the Environment, *This Common Inheritance*, Cm 1200 (HMSO, London, 1990); and C Thomas (ed), *Rio: Unravelling the Consequences* (Cass, London, forthcoming).
2 Rees, op cit, p.38.
3 C Ponting, *A Green History of the World* (Penguin, London, 1991).
4 World Commission on Environment and Development, *Our Common Future* (Oxford University Press, 1987).
5 Ibid, p.8.
6 S C Young, 'Sustainable development at the level of the city', in G Stoker and S C Young, *Cities in the 1990s* (Longman, Harlow, 1993), 64-96. Also see Blowers, op cit.
7. D Pearce *et al.*, *Blueprint for a Green Economy* (Earthscan, London, 1989).

2   GREEN PROTEST

Britain's Commons, Open Spaces and Footpaths Preservation Society is usually cited as the world's first environmental group. In fact several organisations were established in Britain in the late nineteenth century as part of the movement to protect landscapes, ancient monuments and wild birds. The acronym NIMBY – not in my backyard – did not come into common currency until the 1980s. But this nineteenth-century concern led early NIMBYs to use environmental arguments to oppose development where they lived. A typical example is Soames Forsyte. Having made his fortune and moved out of London to hang his art collection in his rural Arcadia, he tried to protect his property from a new mental hospital being built nearby.[1] The second wave of environmentalism came in the late 1960s and early 1970s. This was the time when the campaign against a third London airport was at its height; and when the green critique of contemporary society outlined in Chapter 9 was starting to emerge. This chapter examines the roles of environmental groups in the 1980s and early 1990s, and assesses their influence.

THE RANGE OF ENVIRONMENTAL GROUPS

The emergence of environmental group in Britain has been a gradual process (Table 2.1 overleaf). Today, such groups are many and varied. The phrases environmental movement and environmental lobby are often used as umbrella terms. However, it is important to establish that such terms cover groups with a variety of different concerns.

Chapter 1 surveyed the range of issues that environmental groups address. There are the locally-based NIMBY groups focused on opposition to specific development proposals. There are inner-city tenants' groups campaigning for better environmental conditions. There are amenity groups protecting the countryside. Local civic trusts are interested in landscape and recreational issues. Next, groups like the Council for the Protection of Rural England (CPRE) and the Town and Country Planning Association (TCPA) have developed wider planning concerns. Then there are a number of specialist groups interested in protection of buildings, monuments, or rights of way. Two of the biggest of these focus on wildlife. They are the Royal Society for the Protection of Birds (RSPB) and the Royal Society for Nature Conservation (RSNC). Finally, there are a number of groups like the World Wide Fund for Nature (WWF) which have developed their work in an international context. Some third-world groups address environmental issues, relating them to the problems of the North/South divide described in Chapter 1.

Table 2.1 Establishment of environmental groups in Britain since 1865

1865	Commons, Open Spaces and Footpaths Preservation Society
1877	Society for the Protection of Ancient Buildings
1889	Royal Society for the Protection of Birds
1895	National Trust
1899	Garden Cities Association (later Town and Country Planning Association)
1912	Society for the Promotion of Nature Reserves (later Royal Society for Nature Conservation)
1926	Council for the Preservation of Rural England (later Council for the Protection of Rural England)
1961	World Wildlife Fund (later World Wide Fund for Nature)
1971	Friends of the Earth
1972	Woodland Trust
1977	Greenpeace

Cutting across the categories are a number of more radical groups like Friends of the Earth (FoE) and Greenpeace. They have developed a wide-ranging analysis of the direction they feel society ought to be moving in, given the whole range of international environmental issues. Their memberships grew fastest in the late 1980s. Similarly some ethnic and feminist groups have added environmental dimensions to their campaigns.

The 1980s was a period of spectacular growth for environmental groups.[2] Estimates vary, but it seems that membership in Britain nearly doubled from about 2.5 million in 1980, to about 4.5 million or 8 per cent of the population in 1990. It subsequently appeared to decline slightly. The National Trust has more members than the three main political parties put together. This all meant more resources. Income went up nearly four times during the decade. By 1990 the National Trust received about £56 million per annum; WWF more than £20m; RSPB about £14m; and Greenpeace about £5m.

The main significance of this was that groups could employ more people. This enabled them to widen their activities, expand their research capacity, employ professional fund-raisers and develop their media links. This professionalisation equipped them better for the task of attempting to influence central and local government. Some groups suffered a loss of income in 1992-93. FoE's income dropped by 10 per cent, and it had to cut 26 of its 119 posts.

LOBBYING TO CHANGE BROAD POLICIES

This section analyses the lobbying processes whereby groups try to amend public policy.[3] Site-specific proposals are dealt with later. This section has to be read in the context of the Conservatives' exclusion of environmental groups from consultation processes up to about 1987-88 because of government policies to promote development. The details of this, and the changes that followed Margaret Thatcher's 1988 speeches, are set out in Chapter 5. Figure 2.1 is used to explore the issues. The discussion relates groups to the levels of government identified at the end of Chapter 1.

Figure 2.1 The role of groups in policy making

	Column 1	Column 2	Column 3
International level			
EC level			
National and QGA level			
Local level			

Column 1 = Outsider groups denied access to decision-makers: the 'crying the in wilderness' groups
Column 2 = Groups hoping for elevation to Column 3
Column 3 = Insider groups accorded special consultative status

The most influential groups are those accorded consultative status in Column 3. At the national level – see left of chart – they are automatically consulted by ministers, civil servants and QGAs. Great importance is attached to their views. Groups like the British House Builders' Federation and British Roads Federation are thus accorded 'insider status'. In cases like nuclear power, policy makers and business interests share the same goals. Their dialogue is buttressed by a shared set of underlying values and ideas. The groups mentioned here retained their special consultative status throughout the 1980s.

Those groups denied such status are excluded from ministry circles and left 'crying in the wilderness' in Column 1. They may be asked for their views in a token way, but they remain outsiders. Throughout the 1980s anti-nuclear groups were denied access to decision makers. Consequently, they had to concentrate on media campaigns to generate popular support. Only by such means can groups of this kind hope to be taken seriously by policy makers and achieve consultative status. In the early 1990s, an example of a Column 1 group was the anti-roads campaigning organisation Alarm UK.

The distinction between insider and excluded groups holds good at the EC level where the Commission regularly consults big national environmental groups;[4] and at the international level where WWF is widely respected. On the other hand, Greenpeace is usually excluded from decision-making fora and left in Column 1 campaigning for support. Chapter 4 shows how, at the international level, major groups – or non-governmental organisations (NGOs), as they are often called – are expanding their influence in the post-Rio era of the mid 1990s.

At the local level more and more CPRE branches, civic trusts and wildlife trusts moved into Column 3 during the 1980s. They provide expertise and knowledge for local councils. On the other hand, many of the NIMBY groups opposing developments at specific sites are left crying in the wilderness in Column 1.

There is a key point here. Decisions on many of the site-specific proposals discussed below are pre-empted by broad general policy statements in statutory plans. These are structure and local plans, or Unitary Development Plans in London and metropolitan areas. Groups that develop a regular dialogue with local councils, and climb into Column 3, have more chance of influencing policies in statutory plans.

Taken over a decade, there is a dynamic process of groups moving from column to column, doing better at some levels than at others. At the local level, for example, many greening the city, urban wildlife and local FoE groups have moved from Column 1 through the 'hoping for elevation' stage in Column 2 to Column 3. Where they are taken more seriously it is because the views of senior councillors and officers have evolved. Such groups are seen as having a positive contribution to make. Similarly at the national level, FoE's expertise on recycling means that it has been elevated from Column 2 to Column 3.

It is clear that at the national level environmental groups have gained more influence in some spheres than in others. Agricultural and countryside issues are frequently quoted as examples of significant change. Here, the CPRE, RSPB, and other groups have joined the National Farmers' Union (NFU) and the Country Landowners' Association in Column 3. The NFU's post-war dominance is thus over.[5] In other spheres, however, economic interests remain dominant. On motorway and transport issues Whitehall excludes others from Column 3. Ministers believe the motorway-building programme will lead to jobs and economic growth. They are not interested in contrary views.

Looking at the influence of groups across a range of environmental issues, a confusing picture emerges. The model in Figure 2.1 would have to be researched in detail to draw out definite conclusions. Only some tentative judgments can be made here. It seems that on pollution control, footpath access, minerals, open-cast mining, radioactive waste, contaminated land, and water quality, business interests continue largely to dominate. Yet environmental groups appear to be having more impact in such spheres as recycling, marine waste disposal, green belts, protecting buildings and landscapes, nature conservation, adapting the planning system to take account of environmental issues, and use of derelict land.

THE ENVIRONMENT LOBBY'S CHANGING APPROACH

Four trends stand out from the environment lobby's experience of the last decade. First, employment of research staff and availability of funds to commission studies have encouraged groups to put detailed suggestions to government on how to adapt policy. These studies have also been targeted at parliamentary select committees which expanded their work during the 1980s. The emphasis here is on trying to improve policies. Thus, the RSPB has joined in the process of working out what sustainable development means in practice.

Next, a growing interest in pressurising big firms has developed. Examples are media campaigns to discourage packaging and to encourage green consumerism. There have also been attempts to embarrass ICI into ending CFC production, and Fison's into curtailing exploitation of lowland peat bogs. Greenpeace has taken some polluting companies to court. A third-world dimension has developed here. In the 1980s, a boycott of Nestlé products was organised in protest against Nestlé's allegedly unethical promotion of powdered baby milk in the third world. In some cases relationships with companies became more positive. In the late 1980s, FoE began to work with some companies, showing them how to respond to environmental problems.

Third, Greenpeace and FoE, which were the media stunt *enfants terribles* of the environment lobby in the 1970s, have slowly changed their tactics. During the 1980s they deliberately shed some of their old image, and cooperated more with other groups. An example was concerted opposition to water privatisation.

Finally, a new radical approach emerged. Earth First!, the direct action group, arrived from the USA. There it had developed techniques of disabling machinery whilst trying to prevent clearance of forests and other developments in wilderness areas of the far West. Earth First! members were prominent at Twyford Down in Hampshire, where the M3 extension was approved even though it damaged two Sites of Special Scientific Interest, two scheduled ancient monuments and a landscape designated as an Area of Outstanding Natural Beauty. The security firm, Group 4, was called in to protect the site and machinery from the direct action approach of Earth First!. In some places local members chained themselves to mahogany products and threw away keys so that the wood had to be cut and made useless. The Animal Liberation Front went further, using fire bombs and similar techniques to fight its cause. Such groups aim to damage property, not people.

Some radical groups favour a strictly non-violent approach to direct action which damages neither property nor people. In Bristol, for example, people have climbed into trees to try to prevent bulldozers from clearing sites. Some residents' groups have formed human chains to block streets where joy riders have caused accidents. Their aim is to persuade the council to put road humps in place.

Figure 2.2 sets out a simple spectrum of group behaviour. It illustrates the way in which groups have developed two completely different approaches to lobbying during the 1980s and early 1990s. The two extremes are represented by the radical/populist and moderate/conventional styles. The moderate approach uses established consultation procedures to engage in dialogue with government agencies. By contrast the radical approach favours unconventional tactics like stunts, mass demos and direct action. Radicals stick to their goals and do not make compromises. Whereas moderates cooperate with authority in accepting decisions even if they bitterly disagree with them, radicals are confrontational. Groups that fall at the radical end of the spectrum have much in common with the new social movements (NSMs) outlined at the start of Chapter 3. Being part of the New Politics, they have an underlying ideology that challenges that of moderate, conventional groups.

Figure 2.2 Spectrum of environmental group behaviour

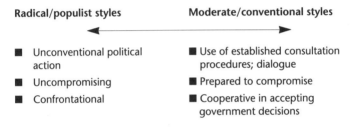

Radical/populist styles	Moderate/conventional styles
■ Unconventional political action	■ Use of established consultation procedures; dialogue
■ Uncompromising	■ Prepared to compromise
■ Confrontational	■ Cooperative in accepting government decisions

In recent years, some populist tactics employed by radical groups have been adopted by groups which have traditionally been very conventional. On countryside issues the CPRE is squarely in the moderate/conventional camp. But in its opposition to motorways in the early 1990s it adopted a much more aggressive profile.

THE IMPACT OF THE ENVIRONMENT LOBBY ON POLICY

The idea of an 'environmental movement' is misleading. It implies common aims, coherence and coordinated activity. The reality is different. Environmental groups have some views in common and a shared sense of what has gone wrong. There is often some agreement about *what* to oppose. But there is a lot of disagreement over *solutions*. It is best to be wary of generalising and to think in terms of an environment lobby with many different strands of thought.

By the early 1990s a paradox had emerged. The environment lobby now has greater resources and a much higher profile than it had in the late 1970s. But it has a limited and erratic impact at the national level. Its influence has been great in spheres of policy like the countryside, mentioned above. But there are other areas in which business interests still predominate. On roads there may be isolated victories like withdrawal of the Oxleas Wood and Hereford by-pass schemes. But the basic policy continues.

The environment lobby can claim, though, that it has helped to educate the public on environmental issues, and to have persuaded the political parties to start to take those issues more seriously. The lobby has also placed detailed topics on the national agenda and propelled some local councils down the environment road. It contributed to the changing climate in which Whitehall received EC directives and reviewed policy during the 1988-93 period. The extent to which groups' ideas are not just permeating government departments but gaining ground within them remains to be seen. In some areas of policy the lobby looks to have better prospects in Brussels.

OPPOSING NEW DEVELOPMENT PROPOSALS

The focus now shifts away from broad policies to what local environmental groups are often confronted with: new development schemes. The initial task is to identify those who will make the decision.

In cases for which planning permission is needed, the issue will usually be determined locally. A meeting of full council is required to approve planning committee decisions. However, the latter is really the key decision-making forum. Here councillors tend to take officers' advice into consideration, but they may disregard it. At this level, the key figures are usually the chair of the planning committee, the Chief Planning Officer, the planning officer actually writing the report that goes to the committee, and local ward councillors. Occasionally, the decision will be made by a QGA, or, for a road scheme, in Whitehall.

The obvious approach once key decision makers have been identified is to lobby them directly. This can be done via letters, telephone calls and meetings. But the most important part of any lobbying activity is the thinking undertaken beforehand. Groups need to invest time in collecting information and working out relevant arguments. The

Environmental Impact Assessment (EIA) system described in Chapter 5 helps groups. Developers now have to publish more information about their proposals before decisions are made.

The central point here is that some arguments will be considered to be relevant and some will not. On the one hand, you cannot oppose a scheme because it trespasses into your neighbourhood. This puts you squarely into the NIMBY category. On the other, you can object to proposals that contradict the statutory plans referred to above.

Unfortunately, between these two extremes there is an area of ambiguity. For example, the speed with which sustainable development ideas are having an impact varies from council to council. In urban areas in the early 1990s some groups successfully opposed development proposals to concrete over their JIMBOB PLACES. In these places people, kids and dogs get up to all sorts of things – Jogging, Insect hunting, Mountain Biking, Ornithology, Blackberrying, Picnicking, Lolloping about, Angling, Courting, Exploring and Sunbathing. Their argument – that such sites were of environmental value to local people – was considered to be important.

Any group's initial aim must be to develop its case so that it can maximise its opportunities when lobbying decision makers. Sometimes data about an alternative site or route may be part of a case. It can be relevant in the case of a pylon route or a reservoir. But it is a red herring in the case of a housing proposal if the owner of the alternative site is not interested. If the proposal goes to a public inquiry, then the quality of a group's case will be tested by the proposer's barristers.

Apart from direct lobbying, the other broad complementary approach is to encourage others to be active so as to bring direct pressure to bear. The first point is to have as many members as possible. This shows the extent of local support, and opens up opportunities for mass demonstrations. Getting good publicity via local or national media can also help. Another useful tactic is to lobby the tiers of government that are not making the decision. Thus a group can try to persuade a QGA like the Countryside Commission (CC) and a local authority to oppose a project being promoted by Whitehall.

Very few decisions relating to specific projects depend on votes in Parliament. However, lobbying a local MP can be useful if he or she agrees with a group's case. Useful information might be gained via parliamentary questions. But the main benefit is that MPs know their way around Whitehall, so groups can benefit from their intimate knowledge of how the system works.

The final point about indirect pressure is legal. If a decision goes against a group, and the group suspects that legal procedures have not been complied with, it has two further options. First, if it can afford it, it can go to court and seek a judicial review. The second option is to go to the European Commission. This happened over seven cases including Twyford Down in the 1992-93 period. However, the EC accepted that Whitehall had ensured the correct application of the EIA system and no progress was made.

There are also situations in which environmentally-damaging activities already exist: a firm regularly polluting a river, for example. The principles discussed above of locating key decision makers and bringing direct and indirect pressure to bear apply in these situations too.

SUCCESSFUL CAMPAIGNS

Many people think that MP+TV = Success. This over-simplifies and leads to poorly-focused campaigns. Four crucial factors determine whether a group's site-specific campaign will achieve its aims:
● **Gaining access to key decision makers** (discussed above)
● **Developing a strong case based on relevant arguments** (also discussed above)
● **Assembling resources** This includes money (to rent rooms for meetings, pay for printing, advertising, phone bills, and so on) and membership. Strong broadly-based local support can be important in persuading decision makers, and it brings access to members' equipment, such as phones, computers, and sophisticated office facilities. Resources also covers skills. Members need a knowledge of the political system at local and/or national levels so that they can identify key decision makers. They need writing and public-speaking skills so that they can marshall their arguments and information to maximum effect. They need fund-raising, press and public relations skills; and on a big campaign, perhaps accountancy and legal skills. Some campaigns last for years, and skills include all the persistence and determination that can be mustered. The resources available to a group determine not just whether it can put a good case to key decision makers, but also the extent to which it can bring indirect pressure to

bear. In practice, groups in wealthy areas can mobilise a more exten-sive range of resources than can most inner-city groups. This is often a key factor in explaining the difference between success and failure.

● **The level of government commitment** There is a world of differ-ence between a local planning application that is testing the water, and a proposal from a determined government agency. Government may be absolutely committed to projects such as an airport extension or a motorway. Similarly, local authorities involved in granting plan-ning permission may stand four-square behind big industrial develop-ment schemes. A group may mobilise resources well, marshall an effective case, and locate key decision makers, but still get nowhere if central or local government commitment to a project is firm. In con-trast to the first three factors, a group has no control over this factor.

THE GROWING IMPORTANCE OF NOT-FOR-PROFIT, THIRD-FORCE ORGANISATIONS

During the period between the mid 1970s and the early 1990s many groups became frustrated at their inability to change the policies of central government and local authorities. As a result many took their own initiatives, and developed their own organisations to run pro-jects.[6] These partnership bodies bring together resources from the public and private sectors, and from various other sources. They have become active in such spheres as housing, education, the arts, muse-ums, training, community centres, and the provision of services for ethnic and other special needs groups.

In the environmental field the commonest examples are community groups carrying out environmental improvement schemes. Some not-for-profit organisations provide services. Examples are community transport and waste recycling projects. One important trend has been the decision of county wildlife trusts and a variety of other organisa-tions to shoulder long-term maintenance responsibilities through nature reserves, canal improvement schemes and landscapes man-aged for recreational and other benefits.

As a breed not-for-profit organisations represent a cross between a pressure group and a QGA. Like a pressure group, they are indepen-dent of government. However, instead of trying simply to influence policy making, they get involved in implementation and in carrying out projects on the ground. Like a QGA, they have access to public-

THE POLITICS OF THE ENVIRONMENT

sector funds, but they can raise finance from a variety of other sources. They are detached from Whitehall like a QGA, but are not subject to ministerial direction. They are not actually new. It is possible to trace examples back to the nineteenth century. The key point is that their numbers expanded significantly during the 1980s.

Detailed research reveals great variety. Not-for-profit organisations operate at different levels. Some, like the Woodland Trust or the British Trust for Conservation Volunteers, work at the national level. Some, like Groundwork Trusts or county wildlife trusts, relate to local authority areas. Most, however, focus at the neighbourhood level. Some are set up by government, but most emerge spontaneously. These not-for-profit partnership organisations operate as a kind of third force. The term third-force organisation (TFO) is preferable to the vagueness of 'voluntary sector'. It also emphasises the notion of a third force to supplement the public and private sectors.

The emergence of TFOs from protest-group politics is significant in several ways. First, councils can steer resources to them and achieve more than they can alone. Next, TFOs promote participation, community development, jobs, and a sense of local pride so that what is done is looked after. Finally, they embody the argument in the Agenda 21 document agreed at Rio (see Chapter 4) that much of the attack on environmental problems needs to be carried out by local groups. One of the attractions of TFOs is that people can use them as vehicles for putting principles of sustainable development into practice. Group protests can thus be transformed into more positive initiatives. This theme is developed in later chapters.

NOTES

1 J Galsworthy, *To Let* (Heinemann, London, 1922). This is volume 3 of *The Forsyte Chronicles*.
2 J McCormick *British Politics and the Environment* (Earthscan, London, 1991), p.34 and ch.8.
3 See, for example, ibid; Y Rydin, *The British Planning System: An Introduction* (Macmillan, Basingstoke, 1993), ch.10; H Ward with D Samways and T Benton 'Environmental Politics and Policy', in P Dunleavy *et al.* (eds), *Developments in British Politics 3* (Macmillan, Basingstoke, 1993); and G Stoker, *The Politics of Local Government*, second edition (Macmillan, Basingstoke, 1991).
4 S P Mazey and J J Richardson, 'Environmental Groups and the EC: Challenges and Opportunities', *Environmental Politics* 1 (1992) 109-28.
5 McCormick, op cit, ch.4.
6 S C Young, 'The contribution of third force, not-for-profit organisations', in Stoker and Young, op cit, 119-50.

3 GREEN POLITICS AND GREEN PARTIES

This chapter looks at the political context of the 1970s from which green parties emerged. It summarises their electoral performance and ideology, and analyses their internal conflicts, the social background of green voters and activists, and the overall impact of green parties. The record of the British Green Party is related to these issues.

THE 'NEW POLITICS'

Green parties were established during the 1970s and 1980s, born in the context of what has been called the 'New Politics'. A number of writers have focused on the growth of new social movements which followed the student protests of the late 1960s. During the next two decades, particularly in western Europe, growing numbers of peace groups, anti-nuclear power groups, women's groups and various environmental action groups objecting to urban renewal, roads and other development schemes emerged. Such protest groups, or citizens' initiative groups as they were called in Germany, were established locally. In a number of cases this led to the creation of national coordinating bodies. Campaigns against nuclear power programmes in Europe were particularly prominent examples of the New Politics.

NSMs were said to be new because they operated in quite different ways from old, established, social movements like trade unions and farming interests. It is possible to draw out five features of NSMs:[1]

● **New forms of political action** Old social movements stuck to traditional methods of lobbying through consultation channels set up by government. NSMs wanted to remain autonomous, and not compromise their principles through dialogue with government. They rejected serving on government advisory committees with their closed relationships with bureaucrats. They emphasised unconventional political action: mass demonstrations, stunts to attract media attention and occasional use of direct action to mobilise public support. Their aim was to influence government through changed public opinion.

● **New forms of political organisation** Those involved in the various peace, women's, environmental and other groups sought to develop decentralised, open, democratic structures whereby members could participate in decision making. Part of their anti-establishment approach was to get away from the centralised, hierarchical way in which old social movement organisations were run.

● **Participation** NSMs were forceful advocates of wider participation in decision-making processes, wanting individuals to be able to influence decisions that affect their own lives and neighbourhoods.

● **New ideology** NSMs mounted a radical critique of the status quo in post-war Europe. They stood for different political goals from established social movements in developed industrial societies. They challenged the existing consensus on economic growth, gender, and military spending. They questioned where economic growth, post-war affluence and materialism were leading. They stressed instead environmental dimensions, different spending priorities, and cultural and quality-of-life issues. This different set of political goals represented a paradigm shift away from the conventional post-war left-right axis, which had focused on redistributive issues, economic intervention, the size of the public sector, and the role of the state.

● **Broad support base** Old social movements, like trade unions, stressed class conflict, and their members came predominantly from one class. By contrast, women's and anti-nuclear groups, and other NSMs, drew support from people with a wide range of backgrounds that cut across traditional class barriers, bringing like-minded people together. Workers and farmers had long defended their own interests. Those involved in NSMs were motivated by broader aims: what they perceived to be the interest of society as a whole, and not just a self-centred, sectarian interest. This reflected their different ideology.

THE EMERGENCE OF GREEN PARTIES

An appreciation of the New Politics setting within which NSMs developed is crucial to an understanding of the birth of green political parties. As Müller-Rommel has pointed out, the ground was fertile because NSMs had made no impact on the policies of socialist parties, which remained wedded to economic growth.[2] Such parties did not want to adopt policies on nuclear power or the environment that might alienate trade union support. This was especially the case in countries where socialist parties were in power. NSMs were also alienated by the centralised, hierarchical way in which socialist parties continued to run their affairs. Differences between socialist parties and NSMs reflected the way in which their ideologies diverged during the 1970s and 1980s.

Socialists' rejection of NSMs' demands led to changes in the party systems in some advanced industrial societies, particularly in western Europe. Some small left-wing parties emerged, or spilt off to pursue NSM aims. More important from the perspective of this book, however, was the emergence of completely new green parties. We look at the situation across the world, before focusing on the British case.

ELECTORAL PERFORMANCE

Information about the birth and evolution of green parties is summarised in Table 3.1 (overleaf). This shows that the first green parties were established at opposite ends of the world in 1972 and 1973: in New Zealand and Britain respectively. Green parties subsequently emerged in almost all advanced industrial democracies, although they were slow to do so in places like Spain and Greece where there had recently been authoritarian regimes.

Although most of the dates when national green parties were established come from the 1980s, many greens fought elections during the 1970s. This reflects the way in which green parties grew from NSMs. Environmental, women's and other groups emerged at the local level, and put up candidates or supported lists of approved candidates locally. National parties were created later. Thus 'green' candidates stood locally in France (Paris) in 1976; in Austria (Salzburg) and Belgium in 1977; and in West Germany in 1977-78. In both Belgium and Switzerland MPs were elected before a national green party had been established. By contrast, in Finland and Italy a strategy based on promoting a broad movement and supporting lists of candidates was favoured above creating a national party.

In eastern Europe communist parties were still firmly established in the 1980s. But the NSM phenomenon emerged there too.[3] During the 1970s opposition to the prevailing regime was tolerated to a greater extent than at any time since the death of Stalin. Broadly speaking, this was the case as long as people stuck to issues, and did not question the basis of the regime. Thus environmental groups were tolerated. They became, during the 1980s, a kind of Trojan horse. People opposing communist regimes could do so 'legitimately' if they campaigned solely on environmental and similar issues. However, once communist hegemony was broken, environmental issues moved down the political agenda as jobs, the cost of living and other topics seen as more urgent by voters and politicians rose to prominence. After the demise of communism, some greens were nevertheless elected in Bulgaria, Czechoslovakia, Estonia and Romania. In June 1993, 23 green parties formed a European Federation of Green Parties.

Table 3.1 Development and recent electoral performance of national green parties since 1972

Country	Foundation of green party	First green MP elected	% vote (seats) last national election	% vote (seats) 1989 EP election
Austria	1986	1986	1990: 4.8 (10)	
Belgium (Ec)	1980	1981	1991: 5.1 (10)	6.3 (2)
Belgium (Ag)	1982		1991: 4.9 (7)	7.6 (1)
Denmark	1983		1990: 0.9 (0)	N/A (0)
Eire	1981	1989	1992: 1.4 (1)	3.8 (0)
Finland	1987	1983	1991: 6.8 (10)	
France	1984		1993: 7.6 (0)	10.6 (8)
Greece	1989	1989	1992: N/A (0)	2.6 (0)
Iceland	1983	1983	1991: 8.3 (5)	
Italy	1987	1987	1992: 2.8 (16)	3.8 (7)
Luxembourg	1983	1984	1989: 7.5 (4)	11.3 (0)
Netherlands	1983	1986	1989: 4.1 (6)	7.0 (2)
Norway	1988		1993: N/A (0)	
Portugal	1981	1987	1991: N/A (1)	N/A (0)
Spain	1985		1993: N/A (0)	2.8 (1)
Sweden	1981	1988	1991: 3.4 (0)	
Switzerland	1983	1979	1991: 6.4 (14)	
UK	1973		1992: 0.5 (0)	14.9 (0)
West Germany	1980	1983	1990: 4.7 (0)	8.4 (7)
Australia	1972	1984	1993: 3.9 (2)	
New Zealand	1972		1990: 6.8 (0)	

Notes
1 It is often difficult to give precise green party poll data because of electoral alliances with other parties. In all cases data refer to explicit green party performance
2 Belgium has two successful green parties, Agalev and Ecolo
3 In the pan-German elections of 1990, east German greens secured 6.0 per cent of the vote and eight seats
Sources F Müller-Rommel (ed), *New Politics in Western Europe* (Westview Press, London, 1989); S Parkin, *Green Parties* (Heretic Books, London, 1989); *Electoral Studies*, vols 8 (1989) to 12 (1993)

Table 3.1 also summarises the broad electoral impact of green parties. The first green MP to be elected to a national legislature was in Switzerland in 1979. Between then and 1988 green MPs were elected in Belgium in 1981, in Finland, Iceland and West Germany in 1983, in Australia and Luxembourg in 1984, in Austria in 1986, in Italy in 1987, and in Sweden in 1988. The first MEPs were elected in the 1984 elections to the European Parliament in Belgium and West Germany. Green parties made a much greater impact at this level in 1989, when they secured election in six EC member states.

What is often overlooked by analysts is the sub-national impact of green parties. Green have been elected to assemblies at *Land* and state levels in federal systems such as Germany and Australia, to regional and provincial assemblies, and to cities and communes. The data on sub-national elections is very scattered. The most significant case at this level is that of West Germany. Between 1979 and 1988 greens surmounted the 5 per cent threshold required for representation in eight out of the 11 *Länder*. But there are others too. By 1990, greens held the balance of power on 40 of the 284 local councils in Sweden, and had representatives on 90 per cent of them.

Green electoral progress has however been slowed down by personality clashes and internal bickering. This is shown time and again by detailed accounts of events in individual countries.[4] It has generated arguments over the way forward, splinter parties, and a diffusion of effort. Sometimes it has prevented a single party from emerging, as in Holland. On other occasions problems have emerged after a single national party had been created, as in Austria. In countries in which a threshold has to be crossed for representatives to be elected under a proportional representation system, two or more parties standing usually mean that no green is elected. One case in which two parties have come to coexist fairly successfully is, however, Belgium. Here Agalev has emerged in the Dutch-speaking, largely Catholic northern half of the country, while Ecolo covers the French-speaking, more secularised, Walloon area in the south. But in Ecolo's case there were long and bitter disputes in the 1970s and 1980s.

IDEOLOGY

The ideology of green parties draws on the NSM experience. One of green parties' distinguishing features – picked out at the start of this chapter – is development of a radical critique that challenges the whole post-war consensus of the main political parties. As green parties became established they developed NSM ideas, emphasising in particular ecological dimensions.

Key green principles are discussed in Chapter 9. The manifestos of green parties draw from them. They question economic growth, look to a non-capitalist and non-socialist future, and emphasise sustainability issues. They stress social equality and minority rights, grass-roots political participation, disarmament, a sharing of wealth and resources with third-world countries, strong environmental controls, and programmes to phase out nuclear power. In seeking to create a different kind of society, green parties are developing a new paradigm, a shift away from the conventional left-right axis.

INTERNAL ORGANISATION AND CONFLICT

One key NSM feature stressed above was their new organisational approach. Those setting up green parties picked up and developed these ideas. They wanted to promote a new kind of politics, to get away from hierarchy, elites, leaders deciding manifestos and reliance on big organisations for funding. They sought to create independent, decentralised, non-hierarchical parties. On the finance side, membership fees and donations – and in some countries state aid – are supplemented in a novel way. Those who are elected often pay part of their salary to party funds. Petra Kelly, the prominent German green, summed up the aim as being to create 'an anti-party party'.

The main theme is participatory democracy. The goal is to create structures to enable all members to be involved in making policy, and in controlling leaders. Decentralisation and branch autonomy are seen as essential if genuinely participatory structures are to be created. Greens want to get away from the strong centralised leadership of conventional parties. Accordingly, many green parties have a number of spokespersons rather than leaders to deal with the media. The British party is an example. Another important principle is time limits on those holding office, both within the party and in a coalition situation where power is shared with other parties. The aim of 'rotation' is to protect the party from careerist politicians.

One factor that has undermined the growth of green parties is publicity given to their internal disputes. Broadly speaking, two kinds of argument have arisen.[5] The first is over policy and ideology, or more specifically over how far to water down principles to attract electoral support. Many greens oppose compromise on the grounds that this will infect the party with conventional political ideas which they aim to destroy. Others argue that it is hopelessly unrealistic to expect to win electoral support with a radical programme. In Germany, the phrase 'Fundi/Realo dispute' has been used to describe this argument. It refers in particular to potential coalition situations in which greens may have to make compromises with other political parties. A variation on the Fundi/Realo issue has occurred in countries like Belgium and France where greens have had to decide whether to work with environmentalists espousing right-wing viewpoints.

The second kind of argument concerns organisational conflict. Green parties emerged as a result of environmental and other NSM organisations merging. Sometimes important issues were not resolved at the start and flared up again later, as the discussion below on Britain shows. In some countries competing parties have been set up.

Some argue that the structures which have been created, stressing participatory democracy, have prolonged and intensified both kinds of dispute. Kitschelt's analysis of the development of Belgian and German green parties shows how cores of activists gradually emerged at local, regional and national levels.[6] These informal elites failed to interact effectively with each other. The lack of strong leadership then led to continuing, and in some cases, paralysing disputes. Communication and coordination were weakened, and the lack of political rewards deterred able people from standing for office.

WHO ARE THE GREENS?

Green voters tend to be young, well-educated, salaried, white-collar urban workers. In West Germany in the 1980s it was 25 to 34 year olds who were the greens' main supporters. In Austria a quarter of all under-25s who voted in 1986 voted green. Green parties also attract more women than men and more graduates from higher education. They do better not in rural areas, but in urban areas where there are concentrations of public-sector professionals. Green voters also tend to have more secular values than supporters of other parties, and to be more interested in and knowledgeable about politics.

A prominent explanation of why people vote green comes from Inglehart's post-materialist thesis.[7] He identifies a silent revolution, arguing that people's attitudes and values have been changed by the era of economic and political stability which followed World War Two.

Rising incomes, higher standards of living, and more readily available and higher levels of education have combined to create a new middle class. Those brought up since 1945 have experienced greater affluence than did their parents in the 1920s and 1930s. A more questioning media has also meant that these people are more sceptical of governments and less closely tied to one political party. As a result, the more affluent new middle classes of the 1970s and 1980s in advanced industrial societies stressed quality of life and environmental issues associated with the New Politics. Inglehart sees these as post-materialist values.

In some countries green parties have been able to exploit the New Politics and the growth of NSMs at the ballot box. Their manifestos reflect the post-materialist values of parts of the affluent middle classes that have grown up since 1945. But part of the explanation for the erratic electoral progress of the greens is that people who are sympathetic to the New Politics do not always vote for new parties. In the 1980s they did so in Germany, but not in Italy or Britain.

Green party activists have broadly the same social background as green party voters. They tend to be young, well-educated and city-based. In his analysis of Belgian and West German green activists in the 1980s Kitschelt argues that this profile contrasts with that of activists in conventional, mainstream parties.[8] He shows that greens tend to have a higher proportion both of women activists and of active members than do other parties. However, only a small fraction of green party voters actually join green parties. Also, turnover of members is high. The complex structures of green parties appear to alienate people. Furthermore, sympathetic idealists are concerned with policy issues and do not want to shoulder administrative tasks. If they join, they tend not to stay long either.

THE BRITISH CASE

Europe's first green party was founded in Britain in 1973 in the context of debate about the *Limits to Growth* report.[9] In 1975, it changed its name to the Ecology Party. In 1985, the name was changed again to the Green Party. The party's record in national and European elections is summarised in Table 3.2. Up to 1987 it made no impact at either level.

Table 3.2 Statistical picture of Britain's Green Party, 1974-93

Election	Seats fought	Av. % of poll	Highest vote	% of total vote	Party members
1974 (G)	5	1.8	3.9		
1974 (G)	4	0.7	0.8		
1979 (G)	53	1.5	2.8	0.1	650
1979 (E)	3	3.7	4.1		2000
1983 (G)	108	1.0	2.9	0.2	4500
1984 (E)	16	2.6	4.7	0.6	
1985 (L)		4.4			
1987 (L)		5.9			
1987 (G)	133	1.4	3.6	0.3	
1989 (L)		4.1			
1989 (E)	79	14.9	24.5	14.9	11000
1990 (L)		8.0			18523
1991 (L)		6.0			10300
1992 (G)	253	1.3	3.8	0.5	
1993 (L)		5.7			5500

Note Dates refer to different types of election: E stands for European elections; G for general elections; L for local elections. The average per cent of poll column refers to average per cent of poll in seats fought
Sources Parkin, op cit; M Robinson, *The Greening of British Party Politics* (Manchester University Press, Manchester, 1992); press sources

However, at the local level it began to make progress. The low voting figures registered in Table 3.2 mask electoral successes. The party built from a few isolated victories in the early 1980s up to 55 local councillors at county, district and parish levels by 1987. In 1988 greens fought 395 seats, with a third of candidates topping 5 per cent of the poll. By mid 1989 the party had one county councillor, 11 district councillors and 90 parish councillors. In addition, membership climbed throughout the 1980s. By 1988, 250 branches had been established across the UK.

The 1989 election to the European Parliament was the electoral high point of the party's first 20 years. It achieved 15 per cent of votes cast. This was one of the highest votes by a green party in a national election anywhere in the world. Under a system of proportional representation, the party would have won 12 (out of 79) seats. Under Britain's first-past-the-post rules, however, it won no seats and was left only with a delegate with observer status in the European Parliament. The election result surprised politicians and commentators who lost no time in pointing out that the party had benefited from a low poll and from protest votes. However, the result gave a boost to Green

Party membership, which climbed to an all-time high of 18 523 in July 1990. It also encouraged other political parties to analyse the limitations of their environmental policies. It was certainly one factor which prompted publication of the 1989 White Paper on the environment. The Liberal Democrats also responded by developing detailed environmental policies for their 1992 general election manifesto.

In the early 1990s the Party's electoral fortunes waned. Opinion poll support fell to below 2 per cent. The 15 per cent vote collapsed at the 1992 general election to 1.3 per cent, as the environment fell down the agenda, materialist issues predominated, and mid-term protest voters returned to their normal parties. However, the party did claim a part share in an MP. It agreed not to oppose Cynog Dafis, the Welsh Nationalist speaker on environmental and agricultural issues, who stood in Ceredigion and Pembroke North. He won the seat, taking 31 per cent of the vote. His campaign was based on the compatibility of green and nationalist ideas at the local level. Initially at least, he asked a great many parliamentary questions on environmental issues. At the local level the Greens consolidated their numbers of seats in the early 1990s, though Table 3.2 shows their average poll falling. Stroud, where they first won a seat in 1986, became the centre of their achievements. By September 1993 they held one county, 23 district and about 110 parish seats.

Leaving the 1989 vote to one side, the backgrounds of those who vote green and those who are active in the party broadly reflect continental European experience. However, in Britain party members are more likely to live in small towns and rural areas than do their counterparts in Europe.

The failure to capitalise on the 15 per cent vote in 1989 reawakened divisions within the party which had lain dormant since the mid 1980s. The dispute was between so-called electoralist and decentralist wings.[10] Early in 1990 electoralists set up a ginger group called Green 2000 to lobby for organisational change. They argued that, given the urgency of the ecological crisis, the party should focus more explicitly on elections, aiming at government within ten to 20 years. This led them to propose organisational changes designed to simplify party structures, strengthen the leadership and facilitate links with the media. They also wanted to tighten up conference voting procedures to allow only party representatives from local branches to vote, rather than anyone who happened to be in attendance.

Decentralists opposed these ideas arguing that the proposed changes were going in the wrong direction: towards the hierarchy and centralisation characteristic of conventional parties. Also they felt that elections were only one way to promote green ideas, and that the party had a role to play in supporting a variety of extra-parliamentary initiatives. For this faction, the way forward is to promote a new decentralised cooperative society by example, by building from the grass roots and supporting all manner of projects and initiatives.

In September 1991 the Green 2000 motion was carried by 1133 votes to 278 at the Wolverhampton conference. However, this victory proved indecisive. Argument continued as financial crisis, rows over sacking the press and campaigns officers, falling membership and poor election results intensified the issues. The Green 2000 motion had set up an 11-member Executive to oversee day-to-day direction of the party, and a 28-member Regional Council to advise the Executive on strategy. During 1992 conflicts arose between the Executive, largely controlled by electoralists, and the Regional Council, dominated by decentralists. The latter fought back in an attempt to reverse and undermine the changes, and to assert control over policy-making processes. In summer 1992, Sara Parkin and five other members of the Executive resigned. Other activists left in 1992-93 as tensions continued and issues remained unresolved.

There are a number of reasons why the Green Party has not been more successful at the polls in Britain.[11] First, there is the obvious lack of help from British election rules. In contrast to other countries where greens have done well, Britain has a first-past-the-post system instead of proportional representation. In addition there is no state funding of political parties in Britain. This first factor has been reinforced by a second: the way in which rival political parties have developed their environmental policies since the Green Party first seemed to threaten them in 1989.

A third factor is the ability of the political system to lower tension over many environmental issues. NSMs have been weaker in countries where there are lots of channels for protest and concessions have been made. In Britain environmentalists have been drawn into consultation procedures, as Chapter 2 showed. Greens elsewhere have avoided this trap and developed green parties with a distinctive ideology. In Britain potential Green Party voters, and those who did not want to be ensnared into dialogue with government agencies or local councils, joined other organisations. These include independent groups like FoE and Greenpeace, and others linked to political parties, like the Socialist Environment and Resources Association.

A fourth factor thus emerges: the inability of the Green Party to attract and retain people protesting about environmental issues. One explanation for this may be the Green Party's radical image. Rival parties like to label the Greens 'lefties'. Faction-fighting and – for British voters – lack of clear leadership have alienated people further. High turnover of members and lack of finance have led to a lack of organisational capacity at election time. The Green Party itself thus becomes a fifth explanatory factor.

THE IMPACT OF GREEN PARTIES

There are different ways of looking at whether green parties have been successful or not:

● **Electoral success** In some countries greens have hardly registered. Spain is an example. However, the Belgian, Dutch, Italian and Swiss cases show that if greens become established they tend to gain a low but fairly solid base, from which point their vote fluctuates. In Germany, after failing to secure election at the first all-German poll in 1990, greens bounced back at the subsequent three *Länder* elections, taking between 6 and 11 per cent of the vote.

● **Impact on policies** In a few cases green representatives have held the balance of power. Examples are Liège in Belgium between 1982 and 1988; Tasmania between 1989 and 1991; and Nord-Pas-de-Calais in France, where a green head of the regional council was elected in 1992. The best-known example is Hesse in Germany, where the Green Party went into coalition with the SPD between 1983 and 1987. It supported SPD budgets and secured funding for various environmental and social programmes. It succeeded in pushing through initiatives on waste and energy. However, in general greens have found it hard to take advantage of such situations, often being out-manoeuvred by more experienced politicians. In Tasmania they agreed to support the Labor administration in return for help for some favoured projects. But they ended up in a situation in which they were blamed for Labor's unpopular policies, while being unable to influence policy making. Lessons seemed to have been learnt in Belgium in 1992-93, when green support for constitutional reform was offered in return for a tax on waste.

● **Impact on the wider political system** Greens have helped to change the nature of environmental debate, influencing other parties, government agencies and groups lobbying governments. In countries where they have been electorally weak the greens' importance has been as part of the wider environmental movement. In Denmark, for example, greens have not prospered electorally but other parties have continued to view the environment as important. This kind of wider role is all that the British Green Party could lay claim to by 1993.

No single assessment of green party impact can be given. In any satisfactory evaluation several dimensions need to be taken into account.

NOTES

1 For an introduction to this literature see R J Dalton and M Kuechler (eds), *Challenging the Political Order: New Social and Political Movements in Western Democracies* (Polity, Cambridge, 1990).

2 F Müller-Rommel (ed), *New Politics in Western Europe: The Rise and Success of Green Parties and Alternative Lists* (Westview Press, London, 1989).

3 M Waller and F Millard, 'Environmental Politics in Eastern Europe', *Environmental Politics* 1 (1992), 159-85.

4 See Müller-Romel, op cit.; S Parkin, *Green parties: An International Guide* (Heretic Books, London, 1989); and the Profile section in *Environmental Politics* 1 (1992) and 2 (1993).

5 B Doherty, 'The Fundi-Realo Controversy: An Analysis of Four European Green Parties', *Environmental Politics* 1 (1992), 95-120.

6 H Kitschelt, *The Logics of Party Formation: Structure and Strategy of Belgian and West German Ecology Parties* (Cornell University Press, Ithaca, NY, 1989).

7 R Inglehart, *The Silent Revolution: Changing Values and Politics Styles among Western Publics* (Princeton University Press, Princeton, NJ, 1977). See also Dalton and Kuechler, op cit.

8 Kitschelt, op cit. See also Dalton and Kuechler, op cit.

9 D H Meadows *et al.*, *The Limits to Growth* (Universe Books, New York, 1972).

10 B Doherty, 'The Autumn 1991 Conference of the UK Green Party', *Environmental Politics* 1 (1992), 292-7; G Evans, 'Hard Times for the British Green Party', *Environmental Politics* 2 (1993), 327-33.

11 See McCormick, op cit; and M Robinson, *The Greening of British Party Politics* (Manchester University Press, Manchester, 1992).

4 INTERNATIONAL DIMENSIONS

Chapter 1 discussed the nature and scale of environmental problems. It highlighted the transboundary nature of issues like global warming and acid rain. One of the key points to emerge was the need for international agreement and action to tackle many environmental issues. There are limits to what national governments can achieve within their own countries. The first real recognition of this came from discussion at the UN Conference on the Human Environment in Stockholm in 1972. Many international approaches to environmental problems have been developed in the years since World War Two.

ATTEMPTS AT INTERNATIONAL AGREEMENT

The first type of approach to environmental issues at the global level comprises intergovernmental agreements. In the mid 1990s, with recent protocols like that agreed in 1987 in Montreal to reduce the use of CFCs in order to protect the ozone layer, these appear quite new. But in fact international treaties have been developing for some time. For example, the International Convention for the Regulation of Whaling was agreed by whaling countries in 1946.[1] The International Whaling Commission (IWC) was subsequently set up. The IWC's initial aim was to manage whale stocks. It was not until 1958 that ethical issues were discussed. The campaign to save the whale emerged in the 1960s, but did not influence debates within the IWC until after the Stockholm Conference on the Human Environment in 1972. Thereafter there was a small group of pro-whaling states: Norway, Iceland, the Soviet Union, Japan, South Korea, Spain, Brazil and Peru. They were opposed by such countries as the USA, France, Britain, Australia and New Zealand. By 1993 the anti-whaling countries had failed to get agreement for a ban. Whaling for scientific research continued.

Another example is the 1959 Antarctica Treaty, which banned territorial claims and allowed signatories to carry out only agreed activities, such as research, in Antarctica.[2] In 1991, an Environmental Protocol was signed to ban mining in the region for the next 50 years. Eight states, led by Australia and France, had favoured a permanent ban to allow Antarctica to become a wilderness reserve. In the end consensus emerged around a renewable ban.

The second approach to international agreement concerns outside pressure on individual countries. During the 1980s non-governmental organisations like the WWF, and some governments in the industrialised democracies, tried to persuade individual governments to change their approaches on specific issues. This was done via direct discussion with the government concerned, in international fora like the United Nations, and through the media. A recurring example was the destruction of tropical rain forests in Brazil. More widespread were attempts to protect biodiversity and outlaw trade in endangered species. Some of this type of activity was directed at the World Bank. It was criticised for lending money to developing countries for schemes that would cause environmental damage.

Attempts to promote agreement and action at an international level thus represent a clearly established approach. During the late 1980s and early 1990s this strategy was developed, involving more governments and becoming more significant. But the outcome of the Rio Summit showed that, as a strategy, international agreements were making only a limited attack on the scale of the problems.

THE EARTH SUMMIT

The United Nations Conference on Environment and Development – or Earth Summit – was held in Rio de Janeiro in June 1992.[3] It came after a big consultation process on environmental issues that reached outside official government circles across the world. There were actually two conferences at Rio. 176 governments sent national delegations to the official event. But more than 20 000 people – representing 6500 NGOs – attended the alternative event. This was run by NGOs like Oxfam, Greenpeace and their counterparts in the South. It was designed to pressurise governments and publicise issues.

To begin with, two specific conventions were agreed. That on biological diversity was signed by 153 governments. America refused to sign, but President Clinton, Bush's successor, did so in April 1993. This convention aims to conserve the huge variety of flora and fauna on the planet. In signing, governments agreed to develop national plans to monitor and help endangered species and improve degraded eco-systems. The convention on climate change was also signed by 153 governments. This focused on reducing greenhouse gases to tackle the issues of climate change and rising sea levels.

Next, a 'Rio Declaration' was agreed. This was a statement of 27 principles to guide economic development and environmental behaviour at all levels from the individual to the nation state. This Declaration was criticised for its blandness. But it marked a recognition of the need to take on board the sustainable development ideas discussed in Chapter 1, and to steer the world economy in a new direction.

Linked to the Declaration was Agenda 21. This is the name given to the global action plan for sustainable development in the twenty-first century. It has 40 chapters, and is divided into four sections. The first deals with the interdependence of environmental problems, and issues like debt, trade, population and poverty. The second focuses on the need to manage physical resources like forests, the land, the sea and so on, while promoting sustainable development. The third examines ways of strengthening the involvement of organisations like industry, NGOs, local authorities, and groups like farmers, women and the poor in the process of working for sustainable approaches. The final section analyses implementation mechanisms and covers issues like funding, the role of technology and education, and institutional development. Each signatory has agreed to produce a national sustainability plan setting out how it will implement Agenda 21.

Finally, there was agreement to create a new UN commission. The UN General Assembly subsequently set up the Commission on Sustainable Development (CSD). Its main tasks are to monitor progress on Agenda 21s, and to hold governments and agencies such as the World Bank accountable for failures to live up to what was agreed at Rio.

Amongst environmentalists and NGOs the Summit was widely condemned as a limited public relations exercise that did not address the key issues: akin to the rich countries moving the chairs around as the *Titanic* sank. Jonathan Porritt was widely quoted: 'I had low expectations, and all of them have been met'. For the poorer South Rio largely represented the rich North defending its own self-interest. The criticisms fell into four main categories.

First, there was the limited nature of the agreements. They were about principles, not action. They were vague and bland. The attempt to produce a forestry conservation convention failed. The result was a non-binding statement of principles. The climate change convention lacked targets and timetables. The production of Agenda 21s was to be non-binding; and the document itself was criticised over some details, and for being repetitive and lacking targets. Second, there was much criticism of the lack of finance. It was estimated by the UN Secretariat that $600 billion per annum would be needed by the developing countries. In fact only $6-7 billion were pledged at Rio, much of it by Japan. Inevitably this will limit the impact of Agenda 21. Thirdly, much debate was couched in free-market terms, the argument being that the World Bank, development agencies and donor governments think in free-market terms. If this continues unchanged it will undermine attempts to promote sustainable development ideas of the kind discussed in Chapter 1. Finally, many critics argued that the South's perspectives had not been addressed. Discussion had focused on short-term issues and failed to tackle long-term problems like population and the spread of deserts. The South failed to persuade Northern countries to commit themselves to allocating 0.7 per cent of their Gross National Product (GNP) to development aid by the end of the decade. Also, the South's idea of a Green Fund to gain greater influence over the nature of environmental aid was rejected.

These are all serious criticisms. They imply that greater change was possible at Rio. Yet students of politics understand how slowly governments move when confronting change. Change is incremental for a number of reasons. These include the need to maintain existing policy, the influence of groups, particularly business interests, and the difficulty in making major short-term changes to expenditure plans. It was always unrealistic to expect Rio to produce a sea-change in the attitudes of all Northern governments, particularly with the 1992 US Presidential election pending.

But positive things did come out of Rio. It was a useful first step, a pause for further thought akin to a driver on a snow-bound motorway thinking about slowing down to a safer speed. To begin with, it had an important educational effect, not just in terms of individuals, but in terms of confronting Northern governments with environmental problems. Next, Rio gave a significant boost to the role of NGOs. Although excluded from inter-governmental negotiations, they were more involved in the preliminary discussions than they had been previously. Inter-continental coalitions of NGOs emerged as individual organisations developed wider appreciations of the inter-connected nature of environmental and economic issues. They have a greater presence on the international stage than before, which augments their standing within individual countries.

Many see the Commission on Sustainable Development as potentially the most significant outcome of the Rio Summit. It provides NGOs with an additional target through which to press national governments on a continuing basis. It also establishes a new forum in which North and South can negotiate environmental issues. Britain has had long experience of being involved in and influenced by negotiations in such an inter-governmental context, albeit at a regional rather than a global level. It is to development of the European Community that analysis now shifts.

THE DEVELOPING ROLE OF THE EUROPEAN COMMISSION

Although the Treaty of Rome was signed in 1957, member states initially showed little interest in the environment. They were preoccupied with economic issues like agricultural and industrial policy. But from 1972 a series of environmental action programmes was established: 1973-76; 1977-81; 1982-86; and 1987-92. A Fifth Programme is to run from 1993 to 1996. Once the Commission had started to address the environment, it quickly built up momentum.[4] By mid 1991 more than 280 items of environmental legislation had been adopted and about 200 directives had been issued. These covered a wide range of environmental issues including water quality, air pollution, chemicals, noise, biotechnology, nuclear safety and protection of birds.

Three important steps were taken in the late 1980s. First, there was the Single European Act. In 1987 this amended the Treaty of Rome and gave the Commission clearer legal competence to act on environmental issues. This amounted to a recognition that environmental issues had overriding importance. It also established a new principle: environmental protection dimensions have to be built into all Community policies. Second, agreement was reached in 1990 to establish a European Environment Agency to collect and assess data, and to help promote effective implementation of Community legislation. Its creation was delayed by failure to agree the location of its headquarters. The third important development in the late 1980s was the emergence of the Commission itself on the international stage. Dealing with transboundary pollution issues within the Community led it to appreciate it had a wider role to play. For example, in the mid 1980s the 12 EC member states produced more CFCs than either the USA or Japan. The Commission moved from reconciling the needs of member states to help draft and implement the 1987 Montreal Protocol on CFCs.

The Commission's growing involvement in environmental issues has had a strong influence on British policy making. National governments have to work out how best to implement the Commission's regulations and directives in the context of their own systems of government. In the early 1990s the Commission published green papers on the urban environment and sustainable mobility. As a result, member states are likely to agree ways in which they should promote less damaging environmental policies in such spheres as energy, water management and transport. This trend of Whitehall responding to Brussels' lead is also reinforced by the drive to create a single European market. If it is to be completed, then all companies in the Community must compete with each other on equal terms. This means, for example, that pollution-control requirements must be the same in Scotland as in Spain. If they are tighter in Germany than elsewhere, then German firms will face unfair competition because they will have to cope with increased costs. Completing the single market will generate more environmental measures as part of the process of standardising economic conditions throughout the Community. These underlying factors mean that there will be continuing pressures from Brussels on British governments in the 1990s.

The Commission does not have an 'eco-police force' to check up on implementation by member states. Instead, it relies on complaints from individuals, groups, companies and local authorities which want to challenge their national governments. When such complaints are received, the Commission asks the government concerned for its view of the matter. If this is considered to be unsatisfactory, it can pursue three further stages. First, it can issue a formal warning. Next, it can issue a 'reasoned opinion' that the member state concerned is in breach of the law. Finally, it can take the case to the European Court. The problem with this final option is that it takes an average of 50 months from the registering of a complaint to a ruling from the Court. But countries like Britain want to avoid appearing before the Court. So the threat itself is a source of pressure, and sovereignty is compromised.

BRITISH SOVEREIGNTY

The sovereignty issue has become a major matter of contention in recent years. It is in fact highly complex. To begin with there are cases where sovereignty has been retained. Forestry policy still seems to be largely determined within Britain, for example. Next there are cases where EC directives push Britain farther than Whitehall wants to go, thus representing some loss of sovereignty. During the 1980s a number of such cases arose. They ranged from the Wildlife and Countryside Act 1981, which implemented wild bird directives, to the Environmental Protection Act 1990 (EPA), which put Britain in line with Community thinking on wastes and toxic chemicals.

In cases where the government is forced to act against its will there is a considerable loss of sovereignty. Water privatisation provides an example. The government's initial aim in 1986 was for the newly-privatised companies to regulate themselves. The CPRE established that it would be illegal under Community law to give private companies pollution control responsibilities. As a result the Department of the Environment (DoE) proposed to create the National Rivers Authority (NRA) as an independent regulatory agency.

On some occasions the government moves ahead of Brussels thinking. An example is the Agriculture Act 1986. This introduced the concept of farmers managing the landscape rather than maximising food production. This pioneering role has not often applied to Britain, but in cases like these a government needs Brussels' approval for its proposals. There is no loss of sovereignty, unless Whitehall is held back over some of the details of what it wants to pursue.

Sometimes there are implementation delays because governments ignore directives. Italy and Belgium often agree to policies they have little or no intention of carrying out. The shooting of migrating birds in Italy is an example. In such cases countries effectively retain their sovereignty. More commonly, though, delays lead to pleas of special circumstances and bargaining with Brussels. A much-quoted example is the 1975 bathing water directive. This obliged governments to designate bathing beaches which would meet stringent pollution standards by 1985. The Commission persuaded Britain to raise its initial number of beaches from the implausible number of 27 first given to 446. However, raw sewage continued to be discharged near many of these. The government hopes all British beaches will meet

European standards by 1995. Here the loss of sovereignty has been delayed. Nevertheless, it has taken place.

Overall there has been a net loss of sovereignty. Much UK environmental legislation is driven by EC directives. Chapter 5 argues that there have been more shifts in areas of policy covered by EC directives than in those neglected by the Commission.

Pressure from Brussels built up throughout the 1980s. During the 1979-88 period Britain was firmly hostile towards the Commission. This reflected Margaret Thatcher's attitude. The change in government policy dates from acceptance of the 1987 directive on large combustion plants. This aimed to reduce acid rain emissions from power stations. Britain spent years resisting pressures on this from groups and the non-EC Scandinavian countries, before suddenly doing a U-turn in 1988. This coincides with preparation of Thatcher's 1988 speeches on the environment. Since then Britain has continued to discover the limitations of its environmental policies in the EC context, and has cooperated more with Brussels. In part this has been an attempt to live down its embarrassing label of 'Dirty Man of Europe'.[5]

PROSPECTS FOR THE 1990s

Complicated changes are to be introduced from 1993 to give the European Parliament more influence on environmental issues as a result of the Maastricht Treaty. When Parliament disagrees with the Council of Ministers there will be lengthy consideration procedures. Qualified majority voting in the Council of Ministers will become the norm on environmental issues. It remains to be seen whether these changes will improve decision-making and reduce the democratic deficit, or cause confusion and delay.

On the global front Britain looks set to play a leading role in the aftermath of Rio. The British government hosted the September 1993 inter-governmental conference on 'Partnerships for Change', held in Manchester. An international NGO conference to mark the second anniversary of Rio is planned for June 1994, also in Manchester. There will be a lot to learn from press analysis of these events, with regard both to international dimensions, and to the seriousness of Britain's approach to sustainable development.

The UN General Assembly established the CSD in December 1992. The UK was one of 53 UN members elected to the CSD. Its first chair is the Malaysian Ambassador. By mid 1993 a detailed work programme had been agreed. The aim is to consider reports from governments in each year from 1994 to 1997 on major issues like poverty, consumption patterns, population, finance, education and environmental capacity building. In addition, it will look each year at government reports on a range of other issues. In 1994, it will consider health, human settlements, fresh water, toxic chemicals and hazardous wastes; in 1995, land, forests, desertification, and biodiversity; and in 1996, the atmosphere and the oceans and seas. In 1997, the CSD will undertake an overall review of progress by governments in preparing and implementing their Agenda 21s, looking especially at how far they are adopting ecologically-sustainable development ideas.

This is an ambitious programme, but it will be well into the mid 1990s before the CSD's significance is revealed. Potentially it has an important role to play in monitoring governments' progress in producing Agenda 21s, and in forcing the World Bank and Northern governments which give aid to be more accountable in relating their programmes to the principles of sustainable development.

During the mid 1990s it seems likely that Brussels will exert more influence on Britain than will global agreements, with their vague targets of the type agreed in Rio. This is because policy makers within the Commission will be working on the concept of sustainable development in considerable detail. It was emphasised in the Maastricht Treaty, and is at the heart of the EC's Fifth Environment Programme (1993-96). In the 1990s, the EC is likely to be centrally involved in turning the abstract concept of sustainable development into detailed practical policies in developed industrial societies. This, however, has to be set in the wider context of delays in ratifying the Maastricht Treaty, confusion over subsidiarity, and collapse of the ERM in July/August 1993. A new balance between the autonomy of member states and further EC involvement has yet to be worked out.

NOTES

1 M Reader, 'The International Whaling Commission', *Environmental Politics* 2 (1993), 81-5; P J Stoett, 'International Politics and the Protection of Great Whales', *Environmental Politics* 2 (1993), 277-303.

2. C Redgwell, 'Antarctica: Wilderness Park or Eldorado Postponed?', *Environmental Politics* 1 (1992), 137-43.

3 Thomas, op cit.

4 D Judge (ed), *A Green Dimension for the European Community* (Cass, London, 1993), which was first published as a special issue of *Environmental Politics*, vol 1 no 4 (1992). See also Rydin, op cit.; and McCormick, op cit.

5 C Rose, *The Dirty Man of Europe* (Simon and Schuster, London, 1990).

5   ENVIRONMENTALISM IN ONE COUNTRY

Chapters 1 and 4 showed that environmentalism is not possible in one country. The aim of this chapter though is to look at the scope of possible action at the national and sub-national levels, using Britain as an example.[1]

ENVIRONMENTAL POLICY FROM
THE NINETEENTH CENTURY TO THE 1980s

Britain pioneered a number of environmental policies in the late nineteenth century. The growth of cities to power the Industrial Revolution highlighted the social consequences of urban expansion. It led, as novelists like Dickens and Mrs Gaskell show, to polluted air, foul drinking water and overcrowded, damp and insanitary housing conditions. Chapter 1 argued that the environment is, in part in the 1990s, a social issue. In the nineteenth century this was also an important strand in environmental policy. One of the first pieces of legislation was the Alkali Act 1863. This created an Inspectorate to regulate acid fumes emitted from the manufacture of sodium carbonate for use in soap and textile production. Table 5.1 (overleaf) shows that a number of other public health and anti-pollution measures followed.

The next significant environmental initiative came after World War Two. A series of Acts in the late 1940s put in place a new towns strategy, a detailed town and country planning system, and measures to protect wildlife habitats and special landscapes like national parks. This approach was consolidated during the next 30 years with control over pesticides, and with initiatives like the Clean Air Act 1956 and establishment of the Royal Commission on Environmental Pollution in 1970. The former tackled air pollution that produced smogs. The latter was created to give expert scientific advice on pollution issues.

The lack of difference between the Labour and Conservative parties during the post-war era was symbolised by the creation of the Department of the Environment in 1970. This was the product of civil service advice prepared for whoever won the 1970 election. It was accepted by Heath, the incoming Conservative premier. Similarly, the

Control of Pollution Act 1974 was proposed by the Heath govern-ment, and enacted by the incoming Labour government under Wilson. Government indifference to the environment continued after the Conservatives' election victory brought Thatcher to power in 1979. For her governments economic issues came first. Her approach was to emphasise the role of market forces. The Conservatives set out to deregulate the economy and roll back the state to give private enterprise greater freedom to expand. The perspective of successive Secretaries of State for the Environment – Heseltine, Jenkin, Baker, Ridley – was that environmental issues act as an obstacle to develop-ment. Ministers saw increased pollution controls as an extra burden on industry that would limit growth. The only major piece of legisla-tion was the Wildlife and Countryside Act 1981. This was introduced largely in response to an EC directive.

Table 5.1 Summary of British and global environmental initiatives, 1848-1988

1848	Public Health Act
1853	First model town at Saltaire
1863	First Alkali Act
1875	A consolidating Public Health Act
1946	New Towns Act
1947	Town and Country Planning Act
	Agriculture Act: system of guaranteed prices
1949	National Parks and Access to the Countryside Act
	Creation of Nature Conservancy Council
1954	Protection of Birds Act
1956	Clean Air Act
1970	Creation of Department of the Environment
	Establishment of Royal Commission on Environmental Pollution
1972	UN Conference on the Human Environment (Stockholm)
	Publication of *Limits to Growth*
1974	Control of Pollution Act
1976	Department of Transport separated from Department of the Environment
1981	Wildlife and Countryside Act
1986	Chernobyl accident
	Agriculture Act
1987	Creation of Her Majesty's Inspectorate of Pollution
	Publication of Brundtland Report
1988	Government agrees to implement EC acid rain directive
	Thatcher's speeches on the environment

However, it would be misleading to suggest that the environmental movement either collapsed during the 1970s and 1980s or that it lacked influence. Vociferous campaigns to oppose the third London airport, the Windscale project and many motorway schemes, and to change the 1981 Wildlife and Countryside Bill, failed. But there were isolated successes. The government abandoned its search for inland nuclear waste disposal sites because of local opposition. Private-sector proposals to build mini new towns in rural areas around the London conurbation at places like Tillingham Hall in Essex and Foxley Wood in Hampshire also failed. In addition, government attempts to streamline the planning system to facilitate development did not advance as far as ministers like Sir Nicholas Ridley had hoped.

MOVING UP THE POLITICAL AGENDA

In the late 1980s, environmental issues leapt up the political agenda. The most important indication of this was two speeches made by Margaret Thatcher in autumn 1988. When addressing the Royal Society in September, she outlined the range of environmental problems, talked about the need to protect the balance of nature, and accepted the idea of sustainable development. A fortnight later at the Conservative Party conference she claimed that Tory philosophy and the case for protecting the environment were the same. She argued that each generation had a life tenancy – not a freehold – on Earth, and a duty to repair damage. She thus announced that her government intended to comply with the terms of its full repairing lease.

During the following 12 months Margaret Thatcher tried to retain the initiative on the environment. She hosted an international conference on the ozone layer in February 1989. She put environmental issues on the agenda of the July 1989 G7 economic summit. She replaced Ridley with Chris Patten as Secretary for State for the Environment. He had much more positive environmental credentials, and appointed Professor Pearce, the bike-riding green economist, as his adviser. Thatcher also chaired the Cabinet committee which prepared the White Paper on the environment eventually published in the autumn of 1990. Finally, an Environmental Protection Bill was included in the 1989-90 parliamentary programme.

Four main factors explain the attention given to environmental issues during the late 1980s:

● **Pressure groups** Groups were active during the 1980s lobbying Parliament over legislation and working through the media to build public support for their causes.

● **Media interest** Journalists went beyond reporting campaigns to investigate issues like dumping of waste at sea, the sickness of seals in the North Sea, the sinking of the Greenpeace boat *Rainbow Warrior* by the French in New Zealand, and suspected leaks at Sellafield.

● **Official reports** These came from the Royal Commission on Environmental Pollution, parliamentary committees and scientific bodies on issues like acid rain and ozone depletion, and added credibility to public concerns.

● **International directives** EC directives, international treaty obligations and the Brundtland Report created external pressures.

The explanation of Margaret Thatcher's apparent U-turn is that she was caught in an environmental pincer movement that proved irresistible. There was a groundswell of public pressure from below, together with international pressure from Brussels and elsewhere. Thatcher, a politician to her fingertips, was concerned about the next election. Her concern was that the record memberships of environmental organisations mentioned in Chapter 2 might transform itself into a significant anti-Tory vote. When the Green Party subsequently won 15 per cent of the vote at the European elections in June 1989 this seemed a possibility. So it seemed right for her to follow her instincts: not just to jump on a moving train, but to try to drive it.

THE MACHINERY OF GOVERNMENT UP TO 1988

Government action in the environmental sphere cuts across departmental boundaries. The main Whitehall departments with an interest in the environment are:

● **The Department of the Environment** This has mainly been a department of local government, responsible for housing, inner-city issues and council finance, although it covers environmental issues like national parks, recreation and wildlife.

● **The Department of Transport** (DTp) Taken out of the giant DoE in 1976, the DTp's energies and expenditure relate mainly to roads.

● **The Ministry of Agriculture, Fisheries and Food** (MAFF) Because it covers many countryside issues apart from farming, fisheries and food while seeking to maximise food production, MAFF has been a constant target for environmental groups.

● **The Department of Trade and Industry** (DTI) The DTI has been responsible for trying to promote growth of industry and services, including polluting sectors like chemicals.

One of the introductory points made in Chapter 1 was the way in which environmental responsibilities are divided between different tiers of government. Below the international level – dealt with in Chapter 4 – and the national level, there are two other tiers. These are, in the British case, QGAs and elected local authorities.

QGAs are set up by Parliament and funded mainly by the Treasury. They are run by non-elected boards appointed by the sponsoring Secretary of State, to whom they are accountable. Their broad functions are defined by Acts of Parliament and their detailed guidelines and targets are set out by their sponsoring department.

In Britain, QGAs have a significant presence in the environmental field. Some promote economic development with environmental consequences. Examples include urban development corporations, similar development agencies in Scotland and Wales and the Agricultural Development Advisory Service. Some, like the Countryside Commission and the British Tourist Authority, promote recreational activity which affects the environment. Some, like British Rail, provide services with environmental dimensions. Some, like the Health and Safety Executive with regard to hazardous materials, have a regulatory role. A more prominent example is Her Majesty's Inspectorate of Pollution (HMIP), which was created in 1987 from a merger of the four inspectorates dealing with industrial air pollution, hazardous wastes, radio chemicals and water quality.

Outside England there are differing arrangements for Wales, Scotland and Northern Ireland.[2] Many of the English arrangements are paralleled in Wales, sometimes via different institutions. The Scottish Office has more independence and supervises policies which are sometimes slightly different.

The striking feature of these arrangements is that until 1988 responsibilities for the environment were divided amongst different departments and QGAs. This weakened the DoE's ability to play a coordinating role and undermined its authority.

CHANGES TO THE MACHINERY 1988-93

When the Conservatives were elected to office in 1979 they aimed to abolish QGAs as part of an attack on wasteful bureaucracy. Instead they ended up creating new ones. In the environmental sphere one of the side-effects of privatisation was the need to create organisations to regulate the new companies. The NRA was set up in 1989 to cover drainage, flood prevention, fisheries, and recreation as well as pollution control. Similarly, the Office of Electricity Regulation (OFFER) was established and is responsible for pollution control and other environmental issues.

A different explanation lies behind dissection of the Nature Conservancy Council (NCC) and the Countryside Commission. These had originally been established in 1949 and 1968 respectively. In July 1989, the government announced it would create Scottish Natural Heritage out of the Scottish parts of the NCC and the CC, and a Countryside Council for Wales from the Welsh parts of the NCC and CC. In England the rump of NCC was renamed English Nature and kept separate from the CC. Vociferous opposition to the destruction of an experienced national nature conservation QGA was met with the creation of a Joint Nature Conservation Committee to cover UK-wide issues. The new organisations began to operate in April 1991. The explanation for these changes seems to be political. The NCC had frustrated ministers during the 1980s as it became more confident in working with environmental groups in opposing development schemes. Its approach to the management of Sites of Special Scientific Interest had also alienated the landowning lobby.

After the 1992 election John Major abolished the Department of Energy. Most of its work went to the DTI, but its environmental responsibilities were allocated to the DoE. In addition, the Ministry of National Heritage was carved out of the DoE. Its responsibilities include historic buildings, ancient monuments and sport.

POLICY DEVELOPMENTS 1988-93

The major policy developments in the period from 1988 to 1993 are summarised in Table 5.2. The government's much-heralded White Paper on the environment – *This Common Inheritance* – was published in September 1990.[3] It listed more than 350 measures already in place. It made various proposals but few new commitments. It did not really address global issues and was criticised for its unimaginative approach by the *Times* and many others. Environmentalists saw it as a missed opportunity. However, it has a definite value as the first comprehensive list of all environmental policies, and as a benchmark against which to judge future changes.

There seem to be three reasons why such a tentative document emerged from the Whitehall machine, in spite of Patten's enthusiasm. First, the government was wary of offending the transport and business lobbies and adding to industry's burdens at a time when an economic downturn was looming. Secondly, the Treasury, the Department of Energy, the DTI, and especially the DTp were all critical of Patten's more radical ideas, such as a carbon tax. Thatcher failed to support Patten when he became isolated. A compromise document thus emerged as short-term considerations dominated. In the end, prospects for inflation, and the value of the soon-to-be-privatised electricity supply industry on the Stock Exchange, over-rode long-term concerns about the planet.

Table 5.2 Summary of British and global environmental initiatives, 1988-93

1988	British government agrees to cut sulphur dioxide emissions
	Thatcher speeches on the environment
	Agriculture Act sets up Environmentally Sensitive Area system
	Introduction of grants to increase wildlife value of woods
1989	Ozone layer conference hosted by Thatcher
	Announcement that NCC to be dismembered
	Publication of DTp road-traffic growth forecasts
	Replacement of Ridley by Patten at DoE
	Creation of NRA
	Publication of FoE's Local Government Environment Charter
1990	Publication of *This Common Inheritance*
	Environmental Protection Act
1991	Establishment of English Nature
	Emergence of changes to planning system
1992	Cynog Dafis elected as green Welsh Nationalist MP
	Abolition of Department of Energy
	Creation of Ministry of National Heritage
	Earth Summit, Rio
1993	Publication of National Sustainability Plan

The major piece of legislation enacted during the 1988-93 period was the Environmental Protection Act 1990. Much of this was a tidying-up measure, extending previous policy initiatives. A ban on stubble burning and stiffer penalties on dropping litter were introduced. Local authorities were given new responsibilities with regard to litter and noise. Dismemberment of the NCC was put in place. Powers were established to ban dumping at sea, and to set up a register of contaminated land. Genetically-modified organisms were dealt with. The Act also covered two much bigger issues: pollution and waste.

HMIP had been formed in 1987 to promote the concept of integrated pollution control (IPC). The aim of IPC is to get away from 'pipe-end solutions'. Limiting air pollution from an industrial process may create pollution problems in one of the other two media, water and land. The point of IPC is to promote an overall solution to each industrial process. Thus, industrialists have to look at production processes as a whole and reduce or prevent pollution into all three media. This integrated approach tries to limit pollution at source.

The 1990 EPA consolidated existing legislation, basing regulations on IPC and the principle that polluters require authorisation. Local authorities were left to deal with straightforward air pollution cases, while HMIP took on complex 'Part A' ones. Where discharges to water are involved it works closely with the NRA. Operators used to be urged to use the Best Practicable Means of limiting pollution. Section 7 of the Act changed this to BATNEEC: best available techniques not entailing excessive cost. In cases where pollutants are released to more than one medium the authorisation controls aim at BPEO: best practicable environmental option. 5500 industrial processes are covered by the EPA. HMIP is developing a rolling programme to cover existing as well as new processes by December 1996. Any breach of legally-binding authorisations incurs a financial penalty.

The other big issue tackled by the EPA was organisation of procedures relating to waste disposal. Almost all British waste is put into about 4000 landfill sites. Waste Regulation Authorities (WRAs) have been established. Some are local authorities and some QGAs. They license sites, inspect old ones, and enforce remedial action where necessary. They also draw up waste disposal plans to compare forecasts of future volumes of waste with site capacity. Where a local authority is a Waste Disposal Authority (WDA) while simultaneously being a WRA, it has to separate out the two responsibilities. This is to avoid corruption, and to promote privatisation through creation of local authority arm's-length companies that compete with the private sector. WDAs also have to promote recycling.

A 'duty of care' was introduced by the EPA. This means that the producer of waste, the disposer of waste and the regulator have a responsibility for the care of material at particular stages in its movement. The aim is to make it easier to identify who is responsible when things go wrong, and to enforce regulations. Penalties include fines and prison sentences.

It is too early to assess the EPA. But since 1979 some pollution problems have got worse and some better.[4] Air pollution levels have improved, partly because of EC directives, and partly because of the bankrupting of old smoke-stack industries. There has, however, been a downgrading of water quality in rivers. This is partly because controls over pollution from sewage works have been relaxed. Estuary water has improved marginally, while progress on bathing beaches has been very slow.

PLANNING AND COUNTRYSIDE ISSUES

In discussing the environment, the town and country planning system is often overlooked by non-specialists . However, the way in which it operates has implications for many different kinds of environmental issue. First, there is the process of preparing plans that determine how land is used. Locations for landfill sites and major housing developments are, for example, selected through this system. Second, there is the process of making decisions about whether new developments like an out-of-town superstore or an industrial estate should be allowed on specific sites.

The DoE changed the way in which plans were made in 1991-92 so that local planning authorities had to take account of sustainable development and the environmental impact of economic activity to a greater extent than hitherto. Documents instructed planners to take greater account of environmental issues like clean air, water quality, landscape conservation, noise and the consumption of non-renewable resources.[5] Planners were also told to develop policies to help combat global warming through their approach to energy and transport. These affect such issues as location of development, transport infrastructure, prevention of coastal flooding, reclamation of land, location of waste disposal sites and a variety of environmental health issues.

The second way in which the planning system was adapted to cope with environmental issues centred on Environmental Impact Assessment. This was introduced in Britain in 1988, following a 1985 EC directive. It was given a statutory basis in 1991. The point of the EIA system is to assess the full environmental impact of a major project before allowing it to proceed. The developer has to produce an Environmental Statement (ES) when seeking permission for a major project. This must describe the scheme, the site and its environment, and assess the effects of the project. This entails analysing its impact on people, flora and fauna, soil, landscape, air, water, climate, cultural heritage and material assets. ESs are mandatory for major projects like oil refineries, power stations, open-cast mines, motorways and waste disposal schemes. There are also a number of discretionary cases in which ESs may be necessary according to the size of the project.

The significance of these two changes will emerge during the mid 1990s. New instructions on plan preparation are working through more slowly than is the EIA system. The significance of the latter is that under the old system developers often used to try to keep as much information back from the public as possible. Under the EIA system they are required to publish it all in advance of a decision for public inspection and debate. In practice the quality of ESs varies. But their introduction is a significant change.

Since 1988, policies towards farming and rural landscapes have been made more sensitive. But the changes were set in train earlier, by the Agriculture Act 1986. This stepped back from the post-war policy of spreading the agri-business gospel, encouraging drainage of marshes and destruction of hedges in order to maximise food production. It introduced set-aside, and established the principle that farming aims must be balanced with recreational needs and the conservation of wildlife and landscapes. A similar statutory duty was placed on the Forestry Commission in 1985. Grants to increase the wildlife value of woodland were introduced before 1988 and extended afterwards. The Agriculture Act 1988 set up the Environmentally Sensitive Area (ESA) system. Under this farmers are paid to manage landscapes for environmental purposes rather than to maximise food production. By 1992, 23 ESAs had been introduced and more were proposed.

Tighter restrictions on development in rural and coastal areas were introduced after 1988. More national parks and Areas of Outstanding Natural Beauty were declared. From 1992, a new system of prior notification was introduced to control the siting and appearance of proposed agricultural buildings.

Some of the changes to agricultural and countryside policies have benefited wildlife. Although some schemes were initiated before 1988, there has been a significant number of extensions and new schemes since then. Examples include ESAs, and the Countryside Premium and Countryside Stewardship scheme. In 1991, the NRA was given new duties to enhance natural beauty and to protect flora and fauna. In the 12 Nitrate Sensitive Areas the use of nitrate-based fertilisers is monitored in an attempt to reduce damage from nitrates leaching into water courses. Policies to protect badgers and hedgerows have been introduced.

However, the situation is clouded by dismemberment of the NCC, and by weak controls over Sites of Special Scientific Interest and a variety of other areas designated as significant for wildlife. Conservation policies have become firmly established in the countryside. But by 1993 they had had a limited impact. This is partly because schemes depend on the voluntary cooperation of farmers, and partly because levels of compensation are not attractive to them.

The department that responded least to Thatcher's 1988 speeches was the DTp. In May 1989 it published figures to show that road traffic would grow by between 83 and 142 per cent by 2025. The Cabinet agreed to increase the road-building programme from £5 billion to £12 billion. The DTp's argument, set out in *Roads for Prosperity*, was that congested motorways were slowing economic growth as deliveries could not be made, busy executives were stranded on the M25, and exports could not reach ports. Road traffic went up from 272 billion vehicle kilometres (bvk) in 1980 to 408 bvk in 1990.

The main focus of transport policy from 1988 to 1993 was continuity: focusing on roads while reducing subsidies to public transport and deregulating it further. This aggravates global warming and other problems identified in Chapter 1. Although it stepped back in 1993 from the projected road through Oxleas Wood in south London, the DTp pushed ahead with the M3 extension across Twyford Down despite intense local opposition during the period 1992-93. In mid

1993, it announced proposals to widen the busiest part of the M25 to 14 lanes. By then it was directing a 15-year road programme worth £23 billion. Some suggest that the DTp is on the way to becoming a state within the state.

INTERNATIONAL DIMENSIONS

Many commentators argue that the only arena in which Thatcher really changed her environmental policies was the international one. This fits with the interpretation that she saw the environment as a policy area in which she could play a prominent role on the world stage.

The evidence relates mainly to acid rain and sea dumping where, after years of prevaricating, Britain suddenly changed its approach. In June 1988, just before Thatcher's autumn speeches, the government agreed to cut sulphur dioxide emissions by 60 per cent by 2003. This fitted in with the 1987 EC directive on large combustion plants and the foregoing discussions. The aim was greatly to reduce Britain's contribution to acid rain from power station emissions. At the Second and Third North Sea conferences in November 1987 and spring 1990 Britain agreed to end the dumping of sewage sludge, industrial waste and fly ash, and to reduce the discharge of substances on the Red List of most dangerous substances.

Complying with international action to tackle the greenhouse effect and global warming proved more difficult for both Thatcher and Major. This is explained partly by the DTp's ability to resist pressure in Whitehall, and to limit Britain's road traffic contribution to reducing carbon dioxide emissions. Britain aims to stabilise these at 1990 levels by 2005. With regard to ozone depletion the intention is to phase out CFCs by the end of the century.

THE ROLE OF LOCAL GOVERNMENT

The role of local government in tackling environmental problems is often overlooked. In fact one of the major themes to emerge from the Rio Summit was the significant role for local governments worldwide in tackling these issues. Some argue that it is decisions at international and local levels that will be important in the future, not at the level of the nation state.

The previous section in fact mentioned a number of reforms which have added to local authorities' powers. In the sphere of planning, waste, recycling, air pollution and noise, and protection of landscapes, their scope for action has been increased. There are environmental dimensions in the spheres of wildlife protection, recreation, transport, housing, working with community groups, the management of landscapes with minimal use of peat and chemicals and various aspects of environmental health. Local authorities have direct powers and opportunities to influence QGAs, firms, farmers, landowners, groups and individuals.

Pioneering authorities like Sutton, Kirklees, Leicester and Lancashire have realised that the environment is an area in which local councils can play a significant role in improving the quality of local living conditions. They have forged a role, despite centralisation, the cuts and loss of power in other spheres.[6]

Local authorities have produced a whole range of documents. These include environmental charters and internal audits which evaluate a council's overall impact on the environment. More ambitious have been state of the environment audits. These have tried to assess local environmental conditions in the widest sense, from drinking water quality to clean air. The most ambitious councils have tried to follow Lancashire in developing environmental action plans. These aim to identify the main problems and set out policies to tackle them.

The role of local authorities has been reinforced by Rio. The Agenda 21 document discussed in Chapter 4 calls on local governments to produce Local Agenda 21s to set out how sustainable development will be promoted in an authority's area. As a result the DoE has strongly encouraged local authorities to draw up Local Agenda 21s by 1996. In effect this will involve following a state of the environment survey with an environmental action plan. Specific mention was made in the Rio documents of the need to involve women, young people and disadvantaged groups in the preparation of Local Agenda 21s.

ASSESSING THE 1988-93 PERIOD

The picture that emerges from this chapter is that Britain has no policy for the environment. During the late 1980s and early 1990s it added an environmental gloss to different aspects of policy. This reflects the evolutionary approach to policy making in Britain which emphasises continuity and gradual change. The slow development of policies on environmental issues during the nineteenth and twentieth centuries illustrates this. After the mid 1980s increased public and governmental attention to environmental issues caused environmental dimensions to be grafted onto many different policies. This was done with some, though still limited, success in areas like acid rain and the protection of rural landscapes from the impact of the postwar policy of maximising food production. Attempts to limit the growth of road transport and to deal with nuclear waste have failed.

NOTES

1 This chapter draws on Rydin, op cit; McCormick, op cit; J Bradbeer, 'Environmental Policy', in S P Savage and L Robins (eds), *Public Policy under Thatcher* (Macmillan, Basingstoke, 1990); N Carter, P Lowe and A Flynn, 'British Environmental Policy: Administrative Traditions under Pressure' in A I Jansen and K Hauf, *Environmental Policy in Western Europe* (forthcoming); and Department of the Environment, *This Common Inheritance: The Second Year Report*, Cm 2068 (HMSO, London, 1992).
2 Rydin, op cit.
3 Department of the Environment, *This Common Inheritance*
4 Ibid, pp.348-54; Rose, op cit.
5 Young, 'Sustainable development'. Also on local government, see P Allen, *Off the Rocking Horse* (Greenprint, London, 1992).
6 Young, op cit. Also see S Ward, 'Thinking Global, Acting Local?: British Local Authorities and their Environmental Plans', *Environmental Politics* 2 (1993), 453-78.

6   A GREEN SOCIETY?

This chapter examines ways in which Whitehall is trying to change individuals' and industry's perceptions of the environmental problems discussed in Chapter 1, in order to promote a more environmentally-conscious society.[1] During the 1988-93 period Whitehall's approach developed considerably. By the mid 1990s it was based on three sets of policies: regulatory standards, financial instruments and the use of exhortation and advisory services.

STANDARDS AND REGULATORY CONTROLS

The traditional way of dealing with factory pollution of the air or a river is to establish standards above which factories cannot pollute. Such regulatory standards have been widely used since the nineteenth century, and are central to the approach of the Environmental Protection Act 1990 and of HMIP and NRA as outlined in Chapter 5. Regulatory agencies set standards of permitted pollution levels and enforce them, using what are sometimes called command and control methods.[2] These regulatory standards are then enforced by agencies like HMIP and the NRA acting as a kind of eco-police.

The Conservatives under Thatcher found this habitual dependence on regulatory controls distasteful because of their wider view of what was wrong with the British economy. One of the key strands of economic policy throughout the 1980s was the need to deregulate the economy and reduce the burden of state control on industry. Ministers felt regulations distracted managers from managing, and got in the way of allowing market forces to allocate resources to promote investment, growth, dividends, jobs and exports to maximum effect. Once they had decided to develop the environment as a priority in 1988 ministers faced a dilemma. The implication was increased regulation to control pollution. This led them to analyse how regulatory standards work in practice.

Several main problems emerged. First, regulation implies the extra cost of running a government agency to enforce standards. Next, managers are left to cope with the extra burden of state bureaucrats interfering with how they run their companies. Finally, regulatory standards are erratic in their impact. Eco-police cannot be everywhere, so firms sometimes escape detection. Also, if the same standard is applied to all in an industry, or along a river, it will be easier for some firms to control their polluting activities than others. This imposes an unfair extra cost burden on some companies.

Ministers drew two conclusions from this line of analysis. First, despite the problems there were circumstances in which regulations provide the most appropriate mechanism. This led to creation of the NRA and the 1990 Act. Their second conclusion was the need to look in more detail at the potential value of alternative methods of reducing industry's impact on the environment.

FINANCIAL INSTRUMENTS

The Pearce Report was at the heart of these debates.[3] It recommended greater use of financial instruments and movement away from reliance on regulatory standards. It accepted the basic argument that firms which respond to market forces degrade the environment because of the externality problem. Thus firms unencumbered by regulatory standards have no incentive to avoid polluting the atmosphere or a river with their wastes.

Pearce's solution was to drive a wedge between the market and the environment. He argued that environmental taxes provide a means of getting decision makers in industry to take into account the damage their firms inflict on the environment when making investment decisions. If the government taxes environmentally-damaging activities, the price of producing goods rises. For managers, the environment becomes an extra cost to be taken into account. As a result investment decision makers look at environmental costs just as they look at labour or distribution costs.

This can be complicated. A straightforward example is a tax on waste going to landfill sites. The cost to industry of disposing of such waste has historically been low. Society as a whole has borne the real costs through rates and taxes. If the full cost of transporting, disposing of and managing a company's waste is paid by the company, there is a stronger incentive on it to reduce the volume of its waste, and to recycle and reuse by-products where possible. Underlying this approach is the principle of using environmental taxes to cajole and encourage firms into action that reduces their environmentally-damaging activities. If taxes are high enough they are forced to react.

Advocates of these financial instruments argue that they have advantages over regulatory standards. They are more flexible. They do not require expensive state machinery to implement, and they are thus more cost-effective. The process of taking environmental costs into account is decentralised from government to the firm, where it is dealt with on a daily basis. Also, using instruments side-steps the need to change attitudes. If environmental costs are included in the price of goods, consumers take the environment into account unconsciously.

However, in practice there are problems. First, wholesale changes add to industry's costs. They affect prices, inflation forecasts, companies' investment plans, and prospects for economic growth. Next, the practicalities of these schemes are often complex. They rely on bureaucrats to monitor them so that they can be adjusted. Third, these are taxes that affect some sectors much more than others. This opens up arguments about fairness, and about whether such taxes should replace existing taxes, or simply be additional.

Lead-free petrol provides the main example of wider use of financial instruments. In 1988, a lower tax was put on lead-free as compared with ordinary petrol. Buying habits changed to such an extent that by 1992 nearly half of all sales were lead-free. Another example is the NRA charging fees for pollution discharges up to permitted levels, while outlawing discharges above those levels.

More unusual was the system of recycling credits introduced in April 1992. When waste is recycled those bodies which would have had to collect and dispose of it save money. The scheme ensures that the council which saves money pays the recycling organisation a credit equivalent to its saving. The credits will help government achieve its target of recycling a quarter of all household waste by 2000.

Financial instruments have also been used in ways that have more in common with interventionist strategies of the 1960s and 1970s than with Pearce. The aim is to provide subsidies to help promote investment in goods and services produced in environmentally-sensitive ways.[4] Farmers have been offered subsidies to help them diversify into timber production. The Non-Fossil Fuel Obligation has been used to offer guaranteed prices to attract investment into the renewable energy sector. Under this scheme electricity supply companies pay a premium price for electricity produced from wind farms and similar projects. Additionally in the 1990-92 period, three government schemes paid out 50 per cent grants totalling £9 million to 50 projects designed to promote innovation in environmental technology.

However, the truth is that during the 1988-93 period there was a lot of interest in wider use of financial instruments, but the extent to which they were adopted was limited. The period was significant for a whole series of consultants' reports, discussion documents and other studies. Road pricing, carbon taxes and a variety of other schemes were canvassed. But the use of financial instruments was more limited than had appeared likely in 1988-89. The extent to which they will be more widely used in the late 1990s is unclear.

Two main principles emerged from the 1988-93 period. First, the government followed a general presumption in favour of financial instruments rather than regulatory standards. Second, the idea that polluters should pay for environmentally-damaging activity became much more widely accepted, both inside and outside Whitehall.

EXHORTATION AND ADVISORY SERVICES

The third group of policies is use of exhortation and encouragement to persuade firms to take environmental problems more seriously. Since 1979, the industrial policies of Conservative governments have been strongly based on the view that government should avoid intervening in industry. Many ministers believe that state intervention in the 1960s and 1970s was a mistake. Effective management is the key to economic growth. One way to tackle environmental problems is to channel information to senior managers in firms of all sizes in services and manufacturing. This third strategy of encouragement and exhortation is based on persuading managers to think and act differently.

This exhortation approach crops up in the media in the form of ministerial speeches and advertising campaigns. It is backed by an extensive range of specialist conferences and seminars, and by a variety of guides. An example is the Energy Efficiency Office's Best Practice Programme to encourage energy efficiency with regard to industrial processes, and the design and management of buildings. One aim is to cut industry's CO_2 emissions. In 1991-92, its first year, 600 big companies and public-sector bodies took part in the 'Making a Corporate Commitment' campaign to persuade directors to set formal targets to improve their energy efficiency. Similar information dissemination approaches have been developed to encourage companies to reduce the volume of their waste.

These schemes are rather haphazard in approach. They depend on companies responding to circulars about a seminar or the 'Corporate Commitment' campaign. The exhortation strategy is supplemented by more specific advisory services designed to engage individual firms in dialogue. The Energy Efficiency Office runs an Energy Management Assistance Scheme aimed at small and medium sized companies. During the 1989-92 period the DTI's Environmental Inquiry Point dealt with about 120 calls a week.

Sometimes the DTI takes the initiative on the exhortation front and tries to be more active in persuading firms to behave differently. Talks were held with the packaging industry in 1992-93 to encourage firms to reduce the volume of packaging material, and to recycle more of it. This kind of approach sometimes leads to voluntary codes of practice, which avoids formal regulatory controls.

ENVIRONMENTALLY-AWARE COMPANIES

From the late 1970s onwards a growing minority of consumers became steadily more interested in goods they could buy with a clear conscience, even if they were not the cheapest. Sometimes this worked in a positive way, as with cosmetics that had not been tested on animals. Sometimes choice was based on boycotting specific companies, as with those that were tangling dolphins in tuna nets or exploiting black labour in South Africa. During the 1980s, a strong environmental strand developed in this ethical approach to shopping.[5] Initially it centred on fitness and diet: on organic vegetables, free-range eggs and health foods free from salt and additives.

Groups like FoE saw this interest in green consumerism as an opportunity to influence company behaviour by persuading people to buy environmentally-friendly goods. Their greatest success concerned CFCs. They encouraged people not to buy aerosols containing CFCs. Consumption of CFCs in Britain halved between 1986 and 1989.

From a slow start, interest in green consumerism grew throughout the 1980s. Its progress is reflected in the success of the Body Shop. It opened its doors to sell cruelty-free cosmetics in 1976. By 1990 it had 150 shops in Britain and 338 abroad. In 1989-90 it generated pre-tax profits of £14.5 million from a turnover of £84.5 million. Organic farming arrived in Ambridge in 1984, indicating that the trend had become significant enough for a soap opera to tap it. Many characters were initially more than sceptical. But, as in the wider society, they subsequently began to take it more seriously.

The real change in public mood came in the 1988-89 period. This developed largely because of two events discussed in earlier chapters: Thatcher's conversion to environmental issues, and the success of the Green Party in the 1989 European elections. A third factor was publication of *The Green Consumer Guide* in September 1988.[6] It sold 350 000 copies in its first year (compared with 2000 copies for a similar book published in 1985).

Not surprisingly, companies began to realise that the changed public mood was creating market opportunities. Lead-free petrol, products using recycled paper, chlorine-free paper products like tissues, energy-efficient washing machines, and CFC-free fridges were amongst the many examples. New companies were launched in this market niche. Ecover developed a range of environmentally-friendly cleaning materials to exploit it. Supermarkets like Tesco and car firms like the Volkswagen group were amongst others that moved to present their environmental awareness and responsibility as a positive selling point.

In 1989 there were many complaints about claims made by companies. As a result FoE introduced a 'Green Con of the Year' award. The EC subsequently established an eco-labelling scheme to help consumers evaluate companies' claims. In Britain companies apply to the UK Eco-Labelling Board, established in 1993, for accreditation. Washing machines and dishwashers are the first goods to be affected.

The changed atmosphere of the 1980s had two further effects on companies. First, they began to look at their overall relationship with the environment. Environmental audits became fashionable. These examine the total impact on the environment of an organisation's internal operations. They cover obvious issues like waste and energy, but also highlight the environmental impacts of many routine decisions, from the purchase of company cars to the use of cleaning agents.

More ambitious firms graduated to analysing the approaches of their suppliers. This was particularly important for retailers. In August 1993, B&Q took a four-page advert in the national press to explain its progress in working out the total impact on the environment not just of its internal operations, but also of suppliers of all its DIY goods. This was significant, as B&Q had been targeted by local FoE groups and others over the sale of mahogany and peat. With regard to these and other goods, the company changed its purchasing policies.

The government has tried to encourage companies to look at their total impact on the environment through the British Standards Institute. It has published BS7750 as a standard for environmental management systems. Its aim is to provide a framework for firms to use when analysing their impact on the environment.

The other main effect on companies of the changed climate of the 1980s was to encourage corporate social responsibility (CSR).[7] The traditional role of companies in a capitalist economy is to maximise profits, but interest in spending money on schemes that did not earn conventional profits grew. CSR includes giving gifts in kind, ranging from bricks to vehicles to community environmental projects, turning sites like worked-out gravel pits into nature reserves, sponsoring wildlife research and major schemes like canal clean-ups, and lending management skills to not-for-profit organisations through secondments and volunteers. CSR covers an infinite variety of schemes. It is significant in providing resources to the TFOs described in Chapter 2.

The roots of CSR go back to the start of the Industrial Revolution. It subsequently fell out of fashion, but interest was rekindled in the 1970s, initially in terms of arts and sports events. Activity expanded into the environmental field in the 1980s. During the 1988-89 period, WWF received one-fifth of its income from sponsorship.

The reasons why companies get involved are a complex mixture of philanthropy and self-interest. But CSR – like environmental audits – creates opportunities for firms to do some image-polishing and present themselves as responsible citizens. The fact that it has become important for growing numbers of big companies to be seen to be responsible in environmental terms is the point to stress.

The overall significance of green consumerism and the greater environmental awareness of companies needs researching. It is easy to point to pioneers, and to the prosecution of laggards. Supermarket shelves sagging under the weight of environmentally-friendly goods appear to indicate a major change. Moreover, much CSR activity has survived the recession of the early 1990s. As firms have become more environmentally conscious, groups have worked with them in tackling problems. WWF helped B&Q to work out the implications of sustainable development for its purchasing policies in the 1990s.

However, it is only profitable companies that can afford to invest in the research that environmentally-aware production requires.[8] This is qualified by the success of FoE's CFCs boycott, and the ability of companies like J Sainsbury to sell environmentally-friendly goods even if they are dearer than their equivalents. But the extent to which environmental awareness is changing practices and investment patterns in firms throughout the economy – as distinct from in a small number of high-profile companies – is yet to be revealed.

Finally a discussion of green consumerism needs to include local exchange trading systems (LETS).[9] These have spread around the world from British Columbia, where the first scheme was established in 1983. In essence, they are barter systems. Lists are circulated of what individual members need and what they can offer. Anything can be included: a skill like plumbing, or simply feeding someone's cat. As it is unlikely that there will be a straight swop of equal value people trade via a central accounting system. This makes it possible to 'earn' by babysitting for one person, while 'spending' on someone else's building skills. An account is kept of each member's credits and debits.

In Britain, there was a spurt of interest in LETS in 1992-93. By September 1993, 130 systems had been established and more were being set up. Each LETS has its own unit of account: bobbins or links are examples. The biggest system, with 230 members, is in Stroud, the local government stronghold of the Green Party, where trade is in strouds. Although small, LETS represents a radical innovation.

POLICIES AIMED AT INDIVIDUALS

This section takes the three headings that were used at the beginning of the chapter with regard to industry, and applies them to individuals.[10] Government policies here include action at all three levels: central, QGA and local.

First there is regulation whereby laws limit behaviour. Fines and other penalties are imposed for non-compliance. Many examples of **regulatory approaches** to make individual behaviour more environmentally sensitive are long-standing. Examples are smoke-control orders to limit pollutants from coal fires, Tree Preservation Orders to protect trees on private land, laws to prevent disturbance of plants and rare birds, fly tipping, and bans on garden hoses during droughts.

Some of these laws were strengthened during the 1980s, as with wildlife protection. Other more recent controls include stricter car emission standards in MoT tests, traffic-calming measures in residential areas, and bans on smoking in public places and on the sale of unauthorised fuels for household fires. During the oil shock of the early 1970s, speed limits were temporarily lowered on major roads.

The outstanding example of the use of **financial instruments** is the differential tax rate on lead-free petrol discussed above. Fitting water meters in new houses also comes into this category. VAT on domestic energy bills was proposed in Norman Lamont's 1993 budget. The balance of the two arguments was rather unclear, but this was presented in part as an environmental tax, as well as being a revenue raiser. The snag with this approach is that it is regressive. The poor spend a disproportionately high amount of their income on energy. They are thus affected more harshly than are those on higher incomes.

The main emphasis of government policy has been on **exhortation and education**. A great deal of advice has been offered to people: how to cut fuel consumption by driving more carefully; how to garden without using pesticides and peat; how to shop with the environment in mind; how to use water wisely; how to save energy at home, and so on. Another approach to exhortation is the provision of facilities to try to encourage new patterns of behaviour. Prominent examples are recycling facilities, cycle routes, and visitor-management projects at tourist honeypots to spread the pressure, thus reducing environmental damage. More ambitious is the attempt to use the planning system to reduce the need for car-borne travel. If industrial estates, office developments and shopping facilities are enticed towards sites with good public transport links, it is possible over time to influence rush-hour travel patterns.

The last approach to exhortation is to give people powers and responsibilities so that they can take the initiative themselves. The EPA 1990 made it possible for individuals to take a council to court for not cleaning up litter. However this appears to have been little used.

What stands out from the 1988-93 period is the limited nature of government initiatives aimed at changing people's behaviour. Most action has been in terms of persuasion, encouragement and cajoling. Leaflets are everywhere. But – as is the case with firms – individuals can be independent and ignore the advice. As in the industrial sphere, there have been studies of how to use financial instruments to change behaviour. Examples include a carbon tax, an energy tax, water meters in houses which do not have them, road pricing, and charging householders for the amount of waste they throw away. But debate of such topics has not led to much in the way of government initiative.

The first tentative steps have been taken towards a green society, but by 1993 they remained pretty tentative. However, this can only be an interim judgment as Whitehall had yet to pronounce on much of what it had been studying. The National Curriculum, with its environmental ingredients, had not been established long enough to have a noticeable impact on individuals' behaviour as they grow up.

NOTES

1 Department of the Environment, op cit.; also see Carter *et al.,* op cit.
2 See for example M Jacobs, *The Green Economy* (Pluto, London, 1991); or D Pearce *et al, Blueprint For A Green Economy* (Earthscan, London, 1989), ch.7.
3 Ibid; Department of the Environment, op cit, pp.33-5, 43, 45, 112 and 121; and Department of the Environment, *This Common Inheritance,* pp.271-8.
4 Department of the Environment, *This Common Inheritance: The Second Year Report*
5 See for example McCormick, op cit, ch.6; Rydin, op cit, pp.306-9.
6 J Elkington, and J and J Hailes, *The Green Consumer Guide,* (Gollancz, London, 1988).
7 M Fogarty and I Christie, *Companies and Communities: Promoting Business Involvement in the Community* (Policy Studies Institute, London, 1990).
8 Rydin, op cit, pp.308-9.
9 *New Economics,* Spring 1993, No.25, 4.
10 Department of the Environment, op cit.

7 IS BRITAIN DIFFERENT?

This chapter briefly compares environmental problems in Britain with those in other parts of the world. It also draws out some of the new thinking being developed in other countries.

BRITAIN'S POST-WAR RECORD

In the early period after World War Two Britain, with its new planning legislation and Clean Air Act 1956, was held to be a leader in environmental terms. However, during the 1960s, 1970s and 1980s governments became more complacent about environmental issues and conditions deteriorated. By the late 1980s Britain had been labelled 'the dirty man of Europe' and was widely criticised.[1] Chapter 5 outlined attempts to improve the position after 1988, and pointed to some initial changes. But in the 1990s Britain is not in the front rank with Germany, Holland and the Scandinavian countries.

One of the clearest examples of how Britain is worse off than other countries is public transport. Holland and other European countries invest more than does Britain in public transport infrastructure and subsidise its operation. Other areas of difference may also be identified. America is an example of a country that manages to designate areas as real wilderness areas and to keep them that way.

There are some issues on which Britain has emerged in a pioneering role. Other EC countries have followed the Environmentally Sensitive Areas approach to farming discussed in Chapter 5. With Denmark and Germany, Britain is amongst the leading investors in wind energy in Europe. Smoke levels in London are below those in Athens, Brussels, Budapest, Copenhagen, Madrid and Warsaw. Levels in Athens and Madrid actually breach the EC standard.[2]

In many respects there are similar environmental controversies in all industrialised societies. Golf courses are criticised the world over for the amounts of water and fertiliser that are lavished on them. There are similar arguments about the future of nuclear power everywhere. About 20 per cent of Britain's electricity is generated from nuclear power. This is about the same as in Canada and the USA, and less than in Belgium, France, Germany, Japan and Sweden. Most of these countries plan to reduce the role of nuclear power in the next decade.[3] In wilderness areas from Vancouver Island to Tasmania there are huge conflicts between business interests and environmentalists. In some of the western states of America people talk not of NIMBYs, but of BANANA: build absolutely nothing anywhere near anybody.

POLLUTION CONTROL MECHANISMS

Chapters 5 and 6 showed that Britain has relied on a system of delegating powers to regulatory bodies and giving them discretion as to how they use them. This is a different style from that employed in America and Europe. There the favoured approach is to set formal levels in legislation and then to enforce them.

The biggest contrast is with the USA,[4] where until 1970 the main focus was on managing the environment as with wildlife protection and national parks. But in 1970 the powerful Environmental Protection Agency was created. This shifted the emphasis onto looking at pollution levels, and onto strong regulation. The Agency has had little discretion while implementing a stream of legislation on such topics as waste, air, water, pesticides and toxic substances. The 1990 Clean Air Act, for example, forced the Agency to take a tough line on ozone-depleting chemicals. It uses the 'best available technology' approach which was picked up by the EC and developed in Britain in the Environmental Protection Act 1990. Britain's use of cost-benefit and EIA approaches have also been influenced by American experience.

The emphasis on regulation in the USA has created problems. Industrialists do not trust regulatory agencies. This encourages the adversarial approach, with frequent recourse to the courts. Environmentalists join in too, being quite prepared to take the Environmental Protection Agency to court. Meanwhile, legislation produces more regulation. In 1992 the Agency – in response to pressure from President Bush – weeded out 88 of its most burdensome rules to help reduce costs to industry. These factors have encouraged a search for financial instruments. This search was reinforced when Bill Clinton became President. His running mate, Al Gore, had written a best-seller about the environment in which he advocated the use of market-based approaches.[5]

Chapter 6 noted the limited use of financial instruments in Britain during the 1988-93 period, despite Whitehall's interest in them. They cover a wide range of measures including environmental taxes, pollution quotas that can be traded between polluting companies, VAT differentiation rates and subsidies. Other countries have gone further. Scandinavian countries use environment taxes. The OECD and the EC are interested in studying their potential. In the USA an attempt was made in the early 1990s to control SO_2 emissions – which cause acid rain – by issuing tradable permits. However, the theoretical advantages did not work out in practice and a market did not develop.

NEW THINKING

While the USA began to grapple with the problem of an excess of uncoordinated legislative controls, two other countries went in a quite different direction. The Dutch and Canadian governments argued it was logical to produce one wide-ranging document which integrates different policy areas and matches aims with implementation programmes.[6] Both are based on the concept of sustainable development, and each is more ambitious than the British 1990 White Paper.

The Dutch National Environmental Policy Plan was published in 1989. It set out environmental policy aims in quantitative terms with targets of improvements to be met by 2010. The implications for government spending policies and for business, farmers and consumers were all set out. It was criticised for not being tough enough on polluting industries. The Canadian Green Plan was published in 1990. Again, its policies were related to specific targets. Rolling implementation programmes were set out together with their funding implications. Each of these plans takes a long-term approach.

In the early 1990s, Germany introduced changes to its waste policies and developed new lines of thinking.[7] Ministers wanted to move beyond waste minimisation and recycling to the redesign of products. To take one example, yoghurts come in plastic pots. It would be more effective in waste-management terms to have biodegradable or reusable pots. From the start of 1993, German companies were forced to retrieve and recycle the packaging in which they transport their products. However, firms cannot cope with the amounts of material being collected for recycling. Ministers want to leap over the recycling phase by minimising waste through redesign.

Meanwhile it is ironic that the collapse of communism in eastern Europe undermined a well-established system of returning and reusing bottles so that the deposit could be reclaimed. The free market has undermined what the West is painfully trying to introduce. In 1992 a Swedish company opened a plant in Hungary to make soft drinks in cartons. This and the import of cans forced many bottle collection points to reduce their hours or even close.

SUSTAINABILITY INDICATORS

Sustainable development has been widely adopted across the world. It is difficult to define and more difficult to implement, as is shown in Chapter 8. One problem is to work out how to measure progress. Part of this is straightforward: whether the amount of land lost to new building is slowing down or not, whether the volume of waste going to landfill is going up or down. It is much more difficult to work out whether a city's net use of finite resources is increasing or decreasing.

A project was started in Seattle, USA in 1990 to involve local people in working out what they felt were the most important indicators.[8] A broad approach to environmental issues was taken. The aim was to involve not just local government, but business and community groups. Wide-ranging discussion produced a list of 100 indicators, which were then refined by a series of civic panels. One of the main points to emerge was the importance of quality of life issues of the kinds discussed in Chapter 9. Seattle is a city which has improved its air and water quality. These indicators did not come out top. Instead, leading places were taken by levels of adequate housing (third), literacy rates (second) and (first) the number of salmon running through local rivers. The exercise showed officials that they had been mistaken about local people's views of key indicators. This reinforces the argument running through this book that it is important to base Local Agenda 21s on participation and community empowerment.

Sustainability indicators are important in two ways. The first relates to individuals living the greener life-styles discussed in Chapter 9. At present many people feel overwhelmed by information about the environment. They do not know whether it is more important to recycle waste, or to avoid a short car journey to the bottle bank which will increase air pollution levels. If a city has a set of sustainability indicators this helps individuals to understand how best to adapt their life-styles to local problems. Indicators are also important because, over time, they make it possible for the authorities to identify which environmental problems are improving and which are deteriorating. They can then prioritise resources and develop new initiatives.

HOW MUCH REGULATION?

California provides a fascinating case study of attempts to strike a balance between personal freedom and environmental considerations.[9] It is the world's eighth biggest economy. Yet growth and materialism have made it one of the most environmentally-conscious societies. It has long been a world leader in generating of electricity from wind and solar power. Yet, paradoxically, it is heavily polluted. Los Angeles has eight million cars and a serious smog problem. A new regulation was thus introduced to the effect that by 2003 10 per cent of all cars sold in California must be pollution-free. The aim is to provide an incentive to produce electric cars. This will be an interesting test case of the extent to which market conditions can be imposed to encourage major changes in industrial production, while retaining consumer satisfaction.

There is a paradox in the Californian approach. The car is central to the freedom and independence of the life-style. However, controls have been extended as the state has developed what are probably the toughest environmental rules in the world. But industrialists complain that this has gone too far. They have to deal with officials from local, regional, state and federal bodies. A company in Los Angeles needs permission from eight different agencies simply to plant a tree. The frustration of having to deal with the profusion of regulatory agencies is reversing the job-creation success story of the 1970s, Silicon Valley. In the 1990s, unemployment in California has stayed 3 per cent above the national average. This was partly because companies left the state complaining about environmental controls. Yet nine other states are copying California's approach on non-polluting cars. California has yet to find a balance between attracting firms and protecting the environment. Yet, as in Germany and Japan, part of the argument for strict environmental standards is that they stimulate economic development.

The experience of eastern Europe provides a complete contrast. Communism sought to exploit natural resources and to invest for expansion despite environmental side-effects. Some of the world's highest levels of sulphur dioxide outputs per head are in the Czech republic, eastern Germany, Poland and Slovakia. Heavy metal levels are very high near steel plants, and Poland's two main rivers are poisoned by water from mining areas. Effective controls are limited, and people have to live in degraded environmental conditions.

A key point concerns the nature of sustainable development. One dimension identified in Chapter 1 was intra-generational equity. This is the idea of economic activity that benefits deprived and well-off groups. Where an existing works is causing pollution – whether it be in Los Angeles or eastern Europe – those in charge often fend off complaints by saying that they cannot afford preventative measures and may have to close. They offer local people a choice: jobs or a poor environment. In most situations – third world cities, developed industrial societies, and countries emerging into post-communism – people fear job losses more than health risks. The same happens around nuclear complexes and toxic waste processing plants. This is another example of the environment becoming a social issue. Intra-generational equity demands that, if the economy is to be truly green, there should be jobs *and* a high-quality environment.

This is another reason why the Californian case is so interesting. A rich, environmentally-conscious society, with an established tradition of regulatory controls, has yet to tackle the air pollution problem of Los Angeles. Its experience will be an important pointer to the extent to which other societies are able to promote sustainable approaches that include the intra-generational equity dimension. This relates to the concept of ecological modernisation discussed in Chapter 8.

NOTES

1 For comparison see J Porritt, *Where On Earth Are We Going?* (BBC Books, London, 1990); Friends of the Earth, *How Green is Britain?* (Hutchinson, London, 1990); Rose, op cit; and T Elkin and D McLaren, *Reviving The City* (Friends of the Earth, London, 1991).
2 *Economist*, 1 February 1992, p.57.
3 *Economist*, 21 November 1992, pp.23-6.
4 D Vogel, *National Styles of Regulation* (Cornell University Press, Ithaca, NY, 1986); and *Economist*, 8 August 1992, p.39.
5 A Gore, *Earth in the Balance* (Earthscan, London, 1992).
6 A Weale, *The New Politics of Pollution* (Manchester University Press, Manchester, 1992), ch.5; J van der Straaten, 'The Dutch National Environmental Policy Plan', *Environmental Politics* 1 (1992), 45-71.
7 *Economist*, 1 May 1993, pp.34-5; and 3 July 1993, pp.38-9.
8 *New Economics*, Summer 1993, p.6.
9 *Economist*, 16 November 1991, pp.117-26; and 17 July 1993, p.42.

8 FUTURE CHALLENGES

This chapter begins by drawing the concept of sustainable development back into the discussion. It goes on to look at two of the main fears people have about the promotion of environmental issues: loss of individual freedom, and prospects for jobs. The future role of industry and its relationship with government and society are then analysed. The chapter closes by focusing on the longer-term issue of different scenarios for the mid twenty-first century.

SUSTAINABLE DEVELOPMENT

The concept of sustainable development was described at the end of Chapter 1. Chapter 4 explained how governments agreed at Rio to prepare Agenda 21 and Local Agenda 21 documents, setting out how they would apply the concept. For people in Whitehall and town halls the difficulty with sustainable development is in operationalising it.[1] They have to develop policies that are consistent with its goals and reflect its eight features. The eight features are reformulated here into five questions. The idea is to use the questions to get a handle on the environmental sensitivity of different policy proposals.

● **What is the scope for reducing the impact of policies on the environment?** This is about minimising the impact of what society does to the air, the land and the water. Before deciding on a new landfill site for waste disposal, it is necessary to be *sure* it is totally sealed so that, for example, leachate will not leak out and damage a neighbouring Site of Special Scientific Interest. Making judgments in relation to this question is difficult as problems are so wide-ranging. What are the environmental costs and benefits of a big out-of-town hypermarket for example? Similarly a judgment about using rape-seed oil as fuel for buses has to consider a wide range of environmental impacts. These include the fossil fuels used by farmers to plough, sow and harvest it, the fertilisers and pesticides used, their run off into water courses, and the energy used in moving and processing the crop. The environmental costs may outweigh the benefits of the new fuel. Cases like this have led people to argue in favour of the precautionary principle: do not proceed with a project unless you are *totally certain* that you understand all its impacts on the environment.

● **What is the scope for reducing the impact of policies on resources?** An example here is designing all public-sector buildings in energy-efficient ways to reduce heating, lighting and other running costs. Similarly building standards could be further adapted to ensure private developers move in the same direction.

● **What is the scope for managing demand to reduce environmental impacts?** It is possible to limit new office and industrial development schemes to sites that can be plugged into public transport networks. If rail links can be made, the movement of goods and people by road is reduced. Deliberately limiting car parking spaces in cities, while promoting park-and-ride schemes, picks up the same theme of controlling and channelling demand.

● **What is the scope for tackling environmental issues by recycling land and materials?** People relate recycling to waste. But it is an important principle that has wide application. In Bristol an old chapel was converted – exploiting the height of the nave – into a mountain climbing training centre. On one Hebridean island a 30-seater coach has been transformed into a greenhouse to grow vegetables. The silo that housed cruise missiles at Greenham Common is being adapted as a bat roost.

● **What is the scope for thinking laterally and tackling more than one environmental problem at the same time?** This is about addressing an environmental problem in such a way that it has compensatory benefits in relation to other issues. A simple case extends the recycling of derelict land. A new office park or industrial development scheme can be designed not just to promote jobs, but also to include wildlife corridors for the wider benefit of the city's ecology. Another example is Combined Heat and Power whereby the burning of waste produces energy which heats adjacent buildings.

It should be clear from these questions that applying the concept of sustainable development in industrialised societies is and will always be very difficult. It requires decision makers at all levels to change their attitudes. Three different kinds of response are emerging.

First there are tokenists. They adopt a few token measures like cycle paths and nature reserves. But they see the environment as an optional extra, an add-on. They do not address the overall impact of councils, QGAs or businesses on the environment in its widest sense.

The second group are purists who argue for a strict interpretation of sustainable development: massive investment in renewable energy and public transport, for example. They are particularly keen to promote the idea of *ecologically* sustainable development. This is development that does not damage the local ecology. For example fishing that does not threaten total stocks is acceptable, over-fishing is not.

In between the two groups are pragmatists. They accept the limitations of tokenism and understand that sustainable development requires a whole new way of thinking, a holistic approach. This means that all the environmental consequences of a policy have to be analysed. However, they argue that while the purists' approach may have value as a goal, it is unrealistic. It may have potential in rural areas, but cities are net consumers of resources. Those running them seek economic growth, and cities cannot be environmentally benign. Pragmatists try to draw from the other two schools and to develop an approach which is as sustainable as they can make it. However they acknowledge that they are constrained to operate within the context of what is *politically* acceptable. Politicians are particularly worried about placing limits on peoples' freedom.

CURBING INDIVIDUAL FREEDOM?

A recurring theme of this book is the voluntarist approach. Chapter 6 stressed the autonomy of householders when faced with environmental issues. No one can *force* them to mend dripping taps, turn the heating down or separate waste for recycling. This presents governments with a huge dilemma. They want to change people's life styles, but they lack the will to *make* people change. Ministers fear the political unpopularity that loss of freedom would generate.

In this context, the most serious issue is probably traffic congestion, especially at rush-hour times. The majority of car journeys are no more than a few miles in length: to the school or the shops and back. Catalytic converters do not even warm up and start to function over such short distances. Attempts to persuade people to use their cars less are clearly failing. Cars have become important symbols of independence and status, and even environmentally-educated consumers are reluctant to adapt their behaviour. Ministers cater for increased demand in public, while wringing their hands in private over where all this will end. They fear that while people tolerate limitations in pedestrian precincts, they would simply refuse to put up with more extensive controls.

In Holland a debate began in 1993 about fitting electronic equipment to cars and allowing owners to drive a fixed number (say several thousand) of kilometres a year. Owners would be free to decide whether to use their kilometres on a daily basis to get to the shops or to save them up for longer trips. Imposing such allowances presents a major problem for governments. Neither in Britain, nor in California, is a mainstream political party prepared to limit people's use of the car.

The comment that relates best to this dilemma comes from Denis Healey. During the 1979 election, when still Labour Chancellor of the Exchequer, he told Sara Parkin who was standing for the Green Party, 'You're quite right of course, but it's political suicide to say so'.[2] Although he was probably speaking about the whole range of Green policies, this exactly sums up the problem. In Britain at least, we have not reached the point at which political parties are brave enough to take the issue on. But it will not go away. It is most likely to be faced in a coalition situation at a time of crisis. Then the political damage would be more limited. In the meantime Whitehall is pressing on with research into road pricing and other financial instruments, in the hope that politicians do not have to face up to the central problem.

JOB PROSPECTS

People fear that promotion of environmental issues will lead to job losses in a situation in which there are already too few to go round. In fact, promoting environmental issues creates enormous opportunities for jobs. The strategy that needs to be developed during the 1990s is to explore the potential for creating jobs that are environmentally sensitive. There is a widespread popular misconception here. 'Green jobs' is often seen as referring to cleaning-up jobs, such as treatment of toxic waste; to production of sandals and beads for ageing hippies; and to cultivation of organic food for a few eccentrics. Yet the scope for green jobs is enormous. The Centre for Exploitation of Science and Technology estimates that in the period 1991 to 2000 the market for new capital equipment, greener products and environmental services is worth £140 billion in the UK; £850 billion in the EC; and over £1000 billion in the USA.

This market includes a variety of goods and services.[3] There is equipment to help firms meet higher standards: pipe-end filters, waste sorting gear and equipment to monitor and control pollution levels in the different media. There are also completely new products that take account of sustainable development principles. Examples include CFC substitutes, non-toxic paints, and wind-turbine generators. Then there are goods such as biodegradable plastics and detergents, adapted to meet demand from green consumers. Finally, there are service sector jobs: consultants advising companies on how to green their production processes, management of waste and water quality, and firms providing training courses to equip companies for the new future. That future will involve opportunities as well as tighter regulations.

Apart from the actual existence of an expanding market as a spur, green jobs can be promoted in two main ways. First, financial instruments – as discussed in Chapter 6 – can be used in the form of subsidies and other inducements to encourage the development of clean technology.[4] Secondly, local authorities and QGAs can select sites and promote them as green technology parks. The key principle here is to attract firms that are linked to each other in productive ways. Thus specialist waste treatment companies and recycling companies can feed off what other local firms throw out. Where one firm's waste is another's raw material, you create closed cycles which reduce total waste and the overall need to move goods about. Where university research facilities and specialist consultancies are added, you also get the creative energy that comes when people and technologies mix in unpredictable ways.

Jobs do not just come from the public and private sectors. The role of the TFOs discussed at the end of Chapter 2 also needs to be brought in here. The market does not always produce firms to tackle environmental problems. Local authorities and QGAs can use the TFO model to tackle local problems.[5] These range from insulating pre-war terraced houses to planting and maintaining community forests.

There are tensions between NIMBYs and those who want jobs. So far our society has not really begun to explore in detail what focusing on the *quality* rather than the *quantity* of economic growth means in practice. This is a key dimension of sustainable development. It should be possible over time to phase out many environmentally damaging jobs and replace them with jobs that 'go with the grain' of the environment.

ECOLOGICAL MODERNISATION

In the 1970s, as interest in the environment grew, debates about limits to economic growth developed. The argument was framed in terms of a purported incompatibility between economic growth and protection of the environment. The issue was seen in either/or terms. Greater protection for the environment was assumed to lead to reduced economic growth. Increased growth was claimed inevitably to mean greater damage to the environment.

Weale argues that in the late 1980s a new perspective on these issues emerged to challenge the conventional analysis of the 1970s.[6] The essence of his case is that prominent politicians, leading industrialists and questioning officials developed the thesis that economic growth could be *promoted* by giving a higher priority to the environment. He finds evidence for this interpretation in the Brundtland Report, the EC's *Fifth Environmental Action Plan* and in a variety of OECD and national government documents. Their thesis is that more attention to the environment enhances economic growth because increased environmental protection creates conditions that are conducive to long-term economic growth. Environmental protection thus becomes a stepping stone, not an alternative, to economic growth. This approach – encapsuled in the phrase ecological modernisation – is underlined by four inter-connected arguments.

First, there is a growing realisation that lack of environmental protection undermines prospects for economic expansion. Industrial development may produce jobs and growth, goods and services, but the experience of the 1970s and 1980s shows that it uses up scarce resources and promotes environmental degradation. This threatens not just the social resources of the community and workforce on which prosperity depends, but the physical resources too. The costs of cleaning up rivers and clearing up asbestos waste sites do not go away. The next generation has to shoulder them. By the time it does so, they will probably have increased, and will certainly divert resources away from the investment priorities that are promoting the next stage of economic growth.

The second strand in the argument is the way in which major companies have come to realise – as explained earlier in this chapter, and in Chapter 6 – that it is in their interests to take environmental issues more seriously. The environmental crisis has created new markets.

This reflects changing consumer demands, and regulatory pressure for higher standards of pollution control. The existence of global markets accentuates company interest in the environment. Realising that consumers look for quality and not just at price, Japanese car manufacturers have produced cars to higher exhaust emission standards than is necessary. Other companies have had to compete and suppliers have had to cooperate. Once pressures are established, perspectives change, as do long-term investment strategies.

Next, ecological modernisation is promoted by the way in which people move to environmentally-attractive areas. Skilled workers in new technology industries want to live in places offering a high quality of life. Weale quotes the examples of Baden-Württemberg and Bavaria. Growing numbers of the new middle classes have moved to these two southern German regions because of environmental appeal. In Britain this process has been growing in the last 20 years. Firms have been relocating away from the inner city and setting up in the more pleasant surroundings of the urban fringe and smaller towns. People have been moving to areas along the M4 corridor and to more rural places like Calderdale between the Manchester and Leeds conurbations. Some work locally while others become long-distance commuters. These are the post-materialist voters discussed in Chapter 3.

The final strand to draw out is the way in which some groups in society are starting to have more influence on government and industry. The growing impact of consumers on what firms produce has already been discussed. Weale also argues that the new middle classes put pressure on local councils to protect the local environment. Shareholders' questions and ethical investment approaches fit in here too.

Ecological modernisation has important implications for the role of government. First, government needs continually to raise environmental standards to bring pressure to bear on industry. Second, it needs to use financial instruments to develop progressive partnerships with firms, as already happens in Germany and Japan. Third, government needs to respond to the demands of environmentally-aware consumers as a means of pressurising companies and further raising environmental standards. Next it needs to develop its exhortation and education role so that children, householders and managing directors become aware of environmental issues. Finally it needs to take an active role and address problems which others fail to tackle. An example is contaminated land where the firm no longer exists.

Over time the development of these roles by government will start to address two of the more intractable problems. Pressure will be brought to bear on environmentally-irresponsible companies to change their approach. These are short-term profit maximisers, as distinct from environmentally-friendly firms. Second, and more difficult, expensive and time-consuming government action needs to address the degraded environmental conditions of places like the inner city from which the new middle classes have moved.

An example of how ecological modernisation is starting to catch on in Britain came in May 1993 with a report from businessmen and environmentalists.[7] It called for a carbon tax and tough regulations to help Britain meet its international obligations to cut CO_2 emissions to 1990 levels by the year 2000. The Secretary of State for the Environment was surprised that leading figures from ICI, BP, Shell and similar firms rejected his call for a softer, voluntary approach. The involvement of companies in the Groundwork movement to improve the environment is another example of this trend.

The ecological modernisation model is useful here because it updates the capitalist model, relating it to the environmental crisis. It reconceptualises the relationship between economic growth and the environment. Also it examines links between government, industry and people in the post-industrial era. It suggests that they will benefit from cooperation. The extent to which it is consistent with the ideas and features of sustainable development presents quite a research challenge. For example, it fits in with the development of green technology parks, but not with roads-based transport policies and long-distance car commuting.

LONG-TERM SCENARIOS

Speculation is always a contentious business. Writers who look 50 or 60 years ahead, to the time when today's school-children will be pensioners, fall into four main groups.

First are the optimists. They accept that there are serious environmental problems, as outlined in Chapter 1. But they argue that it is important to keep them in perspective. Instead of finding the bucket of water half-empty, they find it half-full. They point to the earth's enormous finite resources and see the idea of passing on capital instead of physical resources as a major step forward. They feel that we have only just begun to explore the secrets of rain forests. We have the accumulated knowledge of science and technology behind us, we have the innovatory skills of private-sector management to exploit, and we have the universe to explore. Above all they believe that necessity is the mother of invention.

By contrast, pessimists find the bucket half-empty and fear that the scale of environmental problems is being under-estimated rather than exaggerated. They are particularly concerned by uncertainty surrounding problems like biodiversity and ozone depletion, and by the way issues such as desertification and rising sea levels seem to be out of control. They see the Rio Summit as a failure. They point to the self-interest of governments in the rich North, and their inability to sign international agreements which will have a real impact on environmental problems. For them science and technology is not a magic wand. Even when it provides answers, we have to remember that liberal industrial democracies are not very good at running bureaucracies. The capacity of the modern state to tackle big multi-dimensional problems is frequently called into question.

Thirdly, there is the muddling-through scenario. This is the belief that, although there will be alarms and excursions and we do not know many of the answers, government and technology will be able to cope. The central element in this scenario is the belief that it is very difficult for government to alter policies suddenly and change direction. The realities of political processes, party and group pressures, fixed expenditure plans and electoral prospects all mean that government does not want to offend groups and voters sympathetic to it. It is thus difficult *suddenly* to invest extensively in renewable energy or scale down the roads programme. Ministers and mandarins have to manage policy change slowly and carefully, especially when there are general constraints on spending and competing claims on Treasury funds to address such matters as unemployment and health care. This scenario is epitomised by the figure of Sir Humphrey in *Yes, Minister*. It sees Whitehall adopting some of the ideas of sustainable development and moving slowly towards others via experimental programmes. Environmental disasters may speed up the process of changing tack, but it will be a long slow haul.

The fourth vision of the future is the subject of the next chapter.

NOTES

1 This section draws on Young, 'Sustainable Development'.
2 Parkin, op cit. p.16.
3 See for example D C Gibbs, 'Greening the local economy', *Local Economy*, 1991, 224-39.
4 For detailed examples, see Department of the Environment, op cit.
5 Young, 'Contribution of third force, not-for-profit organisations'.
6 Weale, op cit. pp.30-2 and 75-9.
7 *Guardian*, 8 May 1993.

9 DIFFERENT SHADES OF GREEN

So far the implication has been that all greens think alike, that the world divides into what governments do and what greens think. The central point of this chapter is that greens approach the issues outlined in Chapter 1 from a series of different perspectives. They have different analyses and different visions which take off in quite distinct directions in trying to build a new future that rejects industrialism, whilst pursuing neither a socialist nor a capitalist path. Their future scenarios are different from the three outlined at the end of Chapter 8. This chapter develops from the summary of the New Politics presented at the start of Chapter 3. Just as new social movements relate to a different paradigm, so too do greens.

POLES APART

One of the points made in Chapter 2 was that the environmental lobby is not a coherent movement. Figure 2.2 presented a spectrum of lobbying styles. The idea of a spectrum can also be used to analyse different ideas about how to tackle environmental problems. Transport policy is used here to contrast the views of weak environmentalists with those who hold more radical views.

At one extreme many environmentalists oppose some new motorways while accepting that others should be constructed. They object to what is lost, but feel that some roads have to be built because of the needs of industry, or because of benefits that come to small towns when through-traffic is evicted onto a by-pass. Weak environmentalists hope that technical solutions like catalytic converters, and planting trees to soak up more carbon, will help address the problems. They argue vaguely for more public transport, but have no answer to those who point out that people are so dispersed now that it has become much more difficult to link everybody to public transport.

At the other end of the spectrum are radicals. They argue that when a government is faced with forecasts of huge increases in road traffic it should take strong measures to invest in public transport, to improve facilities for moving freight by rail, and to discourage people from using cars. They feel that a roads-based transport policy causes environmental damage, adds significantly to atmospheric pollution and generates extra traffic. In the long term they would like to see a society in which people and goods move around a lot less.

A number of writers focus on this distinction between radical and weak environmentalists. Porritt uses the terminology of radical dark greens and weak light greens. Dobson places radical ecologism in opposition to weaker environmentalism. The Norwegian philosopher Arne Naess contrasts the radical deep ecology position with the weaker shallow ecology approach.[1] The Dutch speak of green greens and grey greens. The aim of this chapter is to set out the perspective of radical greens, and to contrast it with weaker reformist views.

THE RADICAL ANALYSIS

People who position themselves at the radical end of the spectrum would argue that what is described in Chapters 4 to 8 is fundamentally misconceived for four reasons. First, the reformist approach uses pipe-end technology to treat the symptoms of environmental crisis, not its causes. Radicals are particularly suspicious of technological fixes and relying on experts to come up with cosmetic solutions. Incinerating waste, for example, discourages efforts to reduce waste. Radicals feel experts have made too many mistakes to be trusted. Often we do not actually know what *safe* pollution levels are.[2]

Next radical greens argue that current policies are continuing to head in the wrong direction. For example, in the early 1990s the British government announced that it would spend £350m to widen the M6 from junctions 11 to 16, a distance of 36 miles. Yet it would not provide £700m to upgrade the 640 miles of the West Coast Main Line from London up past the Birmingham, Merseyside and Manchester conurbations to Glasgow.[3] The motorway widening is estimated to relieve congestion for about ten years. For radicals it is therefore the wrong priority, and represents a total misallocation of resources.

The third radical critique of reformism is that contemporary governments do not appreciate the impact of the economy on the environment, and are unable to monitor it.[4] They use measures that fail to pick up the environmental costs of economic activity. Economic growth is measured in terms of changes to GNP. This measures wealth and income flows around the economy. So *any* activity that involves monetary exchanges adds to GNP. In the British case GNP does not distinguish between environmentally-damaging and environmentally-benign economic activity. Sales of pesticides, new cars and new agricultural machinery are seen as indicators of growth and expansion, despite the environmental damage they cause. By contrast, use of soft, instead of hard, woods in the construction industry, investment in energy saving, and moves to organic farming produce environmental benefits. An environmentally-adjusted national income system could show whether economic activity was helping or harming the environment. In the 1980s the Polish economy contracted whilst causing environmental degradation. The theory of ecological modernisation outlined in Chapter 8 would make it possible to promote growth in tandem with enhanced environmental conditions. Another defect in the British system is that it does not draw into national accounts the tangible and intangible environmental benefits of voluntary not-for-profit activity undertaken by TFOs. This inability of governments to pick up the nature and extent of environmentally-damaging activity undermines what they are trying to do.

Finally, and most fundamentally of all, radicals question the whole ethos of growth. They argue that we cannot grow our way out of whatever economic or unemployment crisis we face. There are finite limits to growth and it has other drawbacks which are discussed below. Porritt likens the argument that we can all get richer and grow more and more to trying to put out a fire with petrol.

Radicals see the weak reformist approach as misconceived. For radicals, cosmetic approaches do not alter the fact that we are carrying on with the whole polluting, growth-oriented, car-driven jamboree. For them ecological modernisation is part of the same approach. It is based on high consumption and technological fixes. It does not fully address the futurity, inter-generational equity, or intra-generational equity aspects of sustainable development.

For radical greens the fundamental problem is economics. They feel that, despite developments since Adam Smith's time, economics continues to convince governments that market forces provide the most effective mechanism for allocating resources. Economists assume that the earth's resources are there to be exploited by capital and labour for conversion into profits. Minerals, water, rocks, even endangered species are valued according to the cost of capturing and transporting them. The production process assumes that resource supplies are infi-nite. Attempts to deal with externality problems have been late, lim-ited and weak. Environmental economics has emerged to try to take account of such criticisms. Yet for radical greens, environmental eco-nomics is no improvement. Chapter 6 showed how governments are using financial instruments to create incentives for companies to reduce their polluting activities. But this is still supporting a system based on taking resources and converting them to waste during the production process in order to feed demand and economic growth.

Similarly, radical greens are suspicious of cost-benefit approaches.[5] The formula for assessing a motorway scheme tries to value costs and benefits. Benefits are measured in terms of lives saved, and time saved on journeys. But radical greens argue that there are some things, such as an important wildlife habitat in the path of a road, on which it is impossible to put a value. It is not just a question of the cultural and natural history and the value of the site to local people. There are also the views that get ruined. Radicals, following writers like Sagoff, argue that it is impossible to put a monetary value on some things. For them economists bewitch governments into believing that everything has a market price. They argue for no compromise on this issue, see-ing it as a trap in which it is best not to get ensnared. This topic is a minefield of assumptions, value judgments and prejudices.

In the short term, radicals want a new framework which could assess economic activity in terms of its environmental impacts. Environ-mental taxes would force companies to look for more benign ways of producing goods, minimising energy, waste and pollution. At present waste and transport costs are so low that there is too little incentive for firms to assess schemes in terms of their full environmental impact. Greens feel governments are still treating symptoms not causes, and that until costs are really put up, companies have no incentive to change their approach.

In the long term, radicals want to see fundamental economic social and political change. Trying to improve the existing system will not tackle the causes of the problem. They thus think in terms of a differ-ent paradigm from the conventional left-right axis. When people first look at the environment they see it in terms of, say, pollution of a river. For radical greens, analysis of such cases leads them right through to the need to restructure society. Far from being single-issue parties, green parties have wide-ranging programmes which aim to reorientate and rebuild society. Their goal is a truly sustainable society. By that they mean a society with a steady state economy that can continue indefinitely without harming the planet. This programme is about a different way of thinking from the conventional approaches of the late twentieth century. It aims to move from consumption and competition to frugality and community.

The next section sets out principles on which radicals would like to base a green society.[6] It ranges more widely than the German Greens' 'four pillars' approach of the 1980s: ecology; social concern and social justice; grass roots democracy and decentralisation; and non-violence.

RADICAL GREEN PRINCIPLES

The first of these principles is **protecting the ecology of the planet and ensuring that future development is sustainable**. Ecology is the study of animals, plants and their relationship to the wider environment in which they exist. Ecology is important for greens as it emphasises how all flora and fauna interact with each other and with all that makes up the physical environment of the planet, whether it be insects or whales, rocks or rivers. All the separate eco-systems – mountain forests, estuaries, oceans and so on – fit together like a fragile three-dimensional jigsaw. Humans are part of nature, just one piece of the jigsaw. For greens, the starting point is that we need to protect the ecology of the biosphere as a whole because we are part of it and dependent on it. Greens look at how people interact with nature, while other parties look at how they interact with markets. Greens argue for a holistic approach where human activities work in harmony with eco-systems, and *all* aspects of a proposal have to be considered, not just some of them.

Radical greens conclude from Chapter 1 that humans should stop trying to dominate nature, and that we should change our approach to economic development so that we protect the biosphere from further damage. This leads to advocacy of pollution control, limits on waste, protection of the ozone layer, preservation of biodiversity, and so on. In particular protecting ecology leads to living within the planet's resources, and to the purist interpretation of sustainable development outlined at the end of Chapter 8. Most of the features of sustainable development outlined in of Chapter 1 fit in here, though some are referred to under other principles below. The ones that relate primarily to this first principle are futurity, inter-generational equity, consideration of environmental as well as economic costs of development, emphasis on the quality of economic growth not the quantity, environmental carrying capacities, and the compatibility of development with local eco-systems.

The second principle is **to restructure the economy so that it meets needs not wants**. The aim is to create a green economy by radically reorganising the existing economy so that it serves different ends. At present in industrialised societies everyone wants central heating, consumer durables, designer clothing and a fast car. Greens look at this from the perspective of sustainable development and the need to reduce consumption levels to save resources. They want the economy to be reorganised to meet the needs of all, rather than centring it around making profits and dividends for some.

Everybody needs the basics of food, housing, clothing and running water. Beyond that greens argue that people are persuaded, through advertising and peer pressure, to want lots of things because others have them. Built-in obsolescence ensures that consumer goods need to be replaced frequently. Products that form part of preventative medicine may meet needs, but the slimming industry thrives on wants. A simple example is trainers. A basic pair will meet the need for practical footwear. But many buy those with expensive labels for reasons of status and style. Big discussions open up about what each of us needs to survive and thrive, as distinct from things we want because others have them. People disagree over where a line should be drawn. But the basic point radical greens emphasise is the difference between needs and wants. Economic growth itself damages people. It leads not to personal happiness and fulfilment, but to exploitation and alienation; to those with jobs spending too much time working at things they do not enjoy; and to people over-valuing material goods. Growth feeds wants not needs.

Creating a green economy also relates to work and quality-of-life issues. The third principle is **establishing a different approach to valuing work and changing the way people relate to work**. Greens want to move from a position in which the focus is on the formal economy and paid work, to a situation in which society recognises the value of all the other things people do with their time. This includes such things as looking after children and elderly neighbours, ferrying people to hospital outpatients departments, and working with youth groups. Greens would like to see everybody receive a basic income to reflect the value of all these 'jobs'. People would then be able to choose whether to add to it by doing paid work, or alternatively to spend more time mountaineering, swimming, reading, or whatever. The aim in establishing a new approach to work is to create opportunities for a better quality of life. If pressures that come from the way in which work is currently organised were removed, people would have more opportunity not just for personal fulfilment, but to focus on what they find spiritually fulfilling as well. This approach would also remove the stigma attached to unemployment, and value the work at home and in the community done by those who are supposedly 'out of work'.

The fourth principle is the green economy's geographical dimension. This is **promotion of bioregionalism and local economic self-sufficiency**.[7] Bioregionalism is the idea of people living in harmony with the land, the seasons and what the natural world provides locally. This is what greens admire about Amazonian forest tribes, North American Indians, peoples on the edge of the Arctic, and Hebridean crofters. These peoples have adopted diets and life-styles that are based on what is available locally, with minimal use of finite resources. They live from the earth's surpluses without interfering with the natural processes that produce them.

Although easier to apply to small towns and rural areas than to modern cities, the principle remains. Greens argue that most local bioregions provide the resources needed for food, shelter, clothing, energy and basic manufactures. These can be supplemented by recycling and repairing scarcer goods. The aim is to produce goods for local needs rather than for profit, and to ensure that local development is sustainable. The target is stability, not growth, a steady-state economy which is in equilibrium with ecological rhythms and capacities.

Bioregionalism and local economic self-sufficiency imply less trade and movement of goods. International trade depends on transport systems that lock up resources. Production of heavy goods vehicles, ships and planes uses finite resources, and motorways, harbours and airports are expensive to build and maintain. Year-round supplies of strawberries in northern Europe fulfil a want not a need.

For greens promoting bioregionalism and local self-sufficiency helps to get away from the situation that faced many communities during the deindustrialisation process of the 1980s. During the post-war period mergers and take-overs led to ever bigger companies, many of which became multinationals. As a result, closure or investment decisions at specific sites were taken in boardrooms hundreds of miles away, and even in other continents. The significant point for local people was that industrialisation under capitalism led to a loss of local control over decisions affecting a plant's future.

Promotion of participatory democracy provides the fifth principle. This has two dimensions. It relates first to the concentration of economic power discussed immediately above. Greens argue that those making economic decisions should be accountable not just to local workers, but to local communities. Greens also relate participatory democracy more widely to the exercise of political power by elites, and to the rejuvenation of democracy. Greens want to get away from a situation in which people vote every few years for governments at national and local levels over whom they have no subsequent control. They want to replace these elective dictatorships with participatory systems in which people are much more involved in setting agendas, discussing issues and reaching decisions. Such approaches promote accountability as well as involving people in decisions that affect their lives. Participatory democracy also dovetails closely with the participatory aspects of promoting sustainable development.

The sixth principle is the **promotion of decentralisation**. This draws together aspects of the previous two principles: bioregionalism and local economic self-sufficiency, and participatory democracy. Decentralisation for greens is about 'small is beautiful', 'politics with a human face', and the creation of a less impersonal society. Greens argue strongly the need to get away from large centralised organisations and their alienating effects. Many experience this at work when remote managers decide another round of reorganisation is needed to promote efficiency. The people at the top are often surprised when the centralised, hierarchical system produces not just limited change in performance, but severely lowered morale.

Greens conclude that society needs to be organised on a much more decentralised scale with smaller organisations, settlements and factories. Economic decentralisation is about creating local economies that are more self-sufficient. In political terms it means elected organisations being much less centralised, and structured in such a way as to be nearer the people. Greens think in terms of councils being elected to run villages and urban neighbourhoods, not cities or regions. They believe that small, decentralised, elected organisations will help rejuvenate democracy because people relate much more positively to where they live than to decisions that focus on a bigger area.

This is in fact a radical approach to subsidiarity. It is about locating decision-making at the *lowest possible* level, and is a different interpretation from that of national politicians. During the EC-inspired debate about subsidiarity in the early 1990s, political leaders asserted that decisions should be made at the *appropriate* level, that is the level they thought most appropriate. But subsidiarity can also mean that higher organisations should be subsidiary to, and at the service of, lower ones. For greens, decentralisation has enormous significance. Here we pick up again the theme of action at the local level and at the international level, not at the level of the nation state.

The seventh principle is **control of technology**. Greens are suspicious of technology. They see government spending on defence and nuclear technology as a misallocation of resources. By contrast information technology and renewable energy projects are examples of an environmentally-benign use of technology which has beneficial and predictable effects. What greens want to see is community control of technology organised on a scale that is appropriate to the size of the settlement or the workplace affected.

Finally there is the principle of **egalitarianism**. Greens are critical of the way contemporary society is characterised by inequality of income and wealth, oppression, exploitation and discrimination. It is not just the poorest that suffer, but minorities too. These include ethnic groups, economic migrants, the disabled, the elderly, and young people. Women are often treated as a minority, though in Britain they form the majority. Feminist dimensions link in here.

For greens egalitarianism is not simply about social justice, equality of opportunity, and the improvement of living standards of poorer groups. It is also about removing the causes of problems like crime, drug dependence, insecurity, and so on. Stress on egalitarianism then links back to the quality of life issue discussed earlier. Greater opportunities make it possible for people to lead more fulfilled lives because they are able to develop their abilities not just at work but in everything else they do. Greens believe people will find new and more satisfying values in a society in which they have self-determination and more responsibility and opportunities. Finally, greens want to use non-violent approaches not just as a tactic to help bring about a green society, but also as part of it once it is established.

Just as greens see ecology on a planet-wide basis, so they relate egalitarianism to international issues. They link it to measures to tackle the North/South divide, to destroying weapons of mass destruction, and to other issues discussed in Chapter 1. For greens cultural diversity is an important asset the peoples of the world have in tackling the problems they face. Egalitarianism relates strongly to the intra-generational equity dimension of sustainable development, not just within individual states, but across the world as a whole.

FURTHER DIMENSIONS

An earlier section in this Chapter used the idea of a spectrum as a presentational device to convey the contrast between what were termed radical and reformist green stances. However, such an approach oversimplifies. It ascribes to the radicals a coherence that they lack.

In the literature on green politics different positions are discussed. There are debates about the relationship between socialism and radical green perspectives, about links between feminism and green ideas, and about the coherence of deep ecology. There is also a philosophical dispute about what is termed anthropocentrism. This refers to the focus of sustainable development on humans at the expense of other creatures and the planet itself. There is also an extensive debate about whether a society based on radical green principles would turn out to be totalitarian, anarchist or somewhere in between.

These and other complex arguments are best explored through the writings of authors like Dobson, Eckersley, and Goodin, who present and analyse the views of different protagonists.[8]

STRATEGIES FOR CHANGE

Individuals in a democracy often feel isolated, lacking influence or control over government. What remains to be discussed is the range of extra-parliamentary strategies available to greens, beyond trying to achieve change by voting green.[9]

The first option for people working for green change outside a green party is **to work through the variety of local and national pressure groups** set out in Chapter 2. Preparation of Local Agenda 21s by 1996, discussed in Chapter 5, opens up opportunities for group involvement and influence at the local level. Another tactic is for groups to register formal complaints about the breach of EC directives. In 1990 the Commission received 125 such complaints from Britain, more than from any other member state.

Greens are split over approaches to involvement in group campaigns. First, there is the problem of specialisation. Some believe that those involved need to understand the detail of, say, renewable energy if they are to influence policy. Others argue that greens must never forget the need for a holistic approach and that it is actually dangerous to specialise. The second issue reflects the Fundi/Realo dispute within green parties. Fundis, purists, feel it is a mistake to get sucked into Column 3 in Figure 2.1 because groups then have to make compromises. Realos, pragmatists, are prepared to do this for some, albeit small, gains over policy. They feel it is a mistake when groups are left isolated in Column 1 where they get tempted into direct action, as with the Animal Liberation Front or the Twyford Down cases, because this leads to bad publicity and has negative effects.

The second option for individuals is **to get involved with pioneering projects to show how green ideas work in practice**. Apart from businesses like organic farms, a range of other examples has emerged. The Centre for Alternative Technology in mid-Wales is a prominent example showing how green ideas can be practised in people's homes and gardens in suburbia. Less well-known is the Earth Centre in South Yorkshire near Connisborough. This is a more ambitious educational demonstration project. The first phase should open in 1994 and is partly funded by Brussels.

It is not just high profile schemes that are important. Environmental-improvement projects, recycling schemes, housing coops and other TFOs all, in their separate ways, provide a practical demonstration of green ideas. The LETS system, discussed in Chapter 6, has a similar role to play. At present TFOs tend to operate in isolation from each other. Some see the next stage as encouraging them to work together. The argument is that a neighbourhood development trust, housing coops, a credit union, a city farm, a multipurpose community centre, a LETS scheme, a wildlife group and a range of other not-for-profit organisations could start to trade, barter and interact with each other. Such a strategy could act as a catalyst, promote local neighbourhood control, help restore confidence to run-down communities, and improve opportunities for local people. The Earth Centre aims to act as a catalyst in this way, helping to promote community-based social regeneration in the run-down mining area of the Dearne Valley.

The third way for individuals **to promote green ideas is through the way they live their lives**, and the example they set. One of the longest lists setting out the scope for individual initiative is in *This Common Inheritance*.[10] Examples that relate to life-styles that have not yet been mentioned include shopping at local shops, car-sharing, keeping cars well-tuned, reusing plastic carrier-bags, reporting mains water leaks and pollution incidents, and teaching children about the environment. However, often it is parents who learn from children, especially since the environmental dimensions inserted into the National Curriculum in the late 1980s.

Finally, there are opportunities for individuals to push green ideas through their jobs. Some can promote green ideas because of the nature of their work: in the spheres of pollution control, wildlife protection, environmental sciences and aspects of education for example. Another option is to try to get the organisation for which a person works to carry out an environmental audit and green its internal operations. Much more difficult is taking green ideas into a hostile work situation. In the civil service, local government, the mainstream political parties, and in much of industry and the trade unions, people make decisions on the basis of the conventional wisdom that greens are trying to change. Greens in management, and in professions like town planning, housing, architecture and environmental health operate according to a different paradigm. These are greens in suits who confront conventional ideas with green values on a daily basis. Their significance as a fifth column inside bureaucracies is under-estimated. The extent to which their opportunities to influence decisions and change perspectives has had an impact needs more research.

Greens are strong on analysis of where they would like to be, and weak on how to get there from where we are now. This leads to problems over next steps. Individuals pick amongst the four extra-parliamentary options discussed above. Greens in suits working for county councils go home, change into politically-correct T-shirts and go out to FoE meetings or newt groups. This is the opportunist approach whereby greens try to make waves from the way they run their lives. Individuals adopt green life-styles and try to spread their message, mixing and matching the four options according to temperament.

Other greens strongly disapprove of this haphazard approach, likening it to being lost in a maze without a map. They argue that opportunists lack a *strategy*. It is rather like debates on the British left during the 1960s, 1970s and early 1980s. People argued that it would be impossible to build socialism until there was agreement on ideology, policy and strategy. Only then could the working class vote be mobilised in support of radical change. Similarly many greens argue the need for a clear strategy. One favourite claim is that elections are just one way of influencing people. What is needed is the building of a wider force for change by working with and through the working class, the unemployed and NSM groups. It is argued that this will promote green ideas via other parties, as well as via tha Green Party.

This perspective is said by opportunists and others to be logical, but to lead to endless debate. They see it as unrealistic, over-ambitious and too difficult. Opportunists argue that there is no real alternative to the step-by-step approach, even if short-term compromises have to be made. They accept the limitations of this, seeing some gain as more positive than unending debate. The fact that government is, as Chapters 6 and 8 showed, trying to change people's life-styles via regulation, financial inducement and education is pushing things along in the right direction. Strategists dismiss all this as tokenism.

Many radicals argue that this debate between opportunists and strategists misses the point. They maintain that wider social change will not take place until individuals change. Political debate, government initiative and the four options discussed above only scratch the surface. The real issue is human nature and the selfish and self-centred way people are, as the philosopher Thomas Hobbes argued in the seventeenth century. A green society will only emerge when people fulfil their needs, not their wants. An environmentally-conscious consumer movement for example offers marginal gains. Imports of mahogany into Britain may have been halved between 1988 and 1992, but for radical greens what really matters is reducing overall consumption.

This argument leads some greens to conclude that real change depends on reaching the psyche: we need to get away from lusting after consumer goods and following the dictates of fashion. Only when society moves away from materialism as fulfilment will values that underlie green concepts of a sustainable society begin to emerge.

This leads greens to argue that humans can reach a deeper and more satisfying level of fulfilment by exploring spiritual dimensions. This may involve any number of things apart from religion: spending time with friends, sharing poetry, or walking in a wood to feel the approach of spring. Greens point to community arts environmental projects, arguing that they play an important role not just in raising awareness, but also in opposing the materialist basis of contemporary society. Yorkshire and Humberside Arts supports projects to give children, and in all probability their parents, hands-on experience of environmental issues and an insight into the understanding and fulfilment that come from spiritual dimensions. Greens argue that life cannot be fulfilling if defined in economic terms; and that an essential part of being green is having some kind of spiritual outlet.

NOTES

1 A Dobson, *Green Political Thought* (Unwin Hyman, London, 1990), ch.1.
2 Rydin, op cit, pp.348-9.
3 *Greater Manchester CVS Transport Bulletin*, September 1993, p.5.
4 See V Anderson, *Alternative Economic Indicators* (Routledge, London, 1991).
5 Contrast Jacobs, op cit; and J P Barde and D W Pearce, *Valuing the Environment* (Earthscan, London, 1991). Also see M Sagoff, *The Economy of the Earth* (Cambridge University Press, Cambridge, 1988).
6 The best way into this complex issue is via the appendix in R E Goodin, *Green Political Theory* (Polity Press, Cambridge, 1992), pp.181-203. He takes three green party programmes, looks at what they have in common and relates his interpretation to the ideas of other prominent writers. Some parts of his main text are also relevant to this discussion: decentralisation for example.
7 P Ekins *et al*, Wealth *Beyond Measure* (Gaia, London, 1992); H Daly, *Steady State Economics*, second edition (Earthscan, London, 1992); H Daly and J Cobb, *For the Common Good* (Green Print, London, 1990); and J Porritt, *Seeing Green* (Blackwell, Oxford, 1984).
8 See Dobson, op cit; Goodin, op cit; and R Eckersley, *Environmentalism and Political Theory* (UCL Press, London, 1992).
9 See for example Dobson, op cit; J Porritt and M Winner, *The Coming of the Greens* (Fontana, London, 1988); S Irvine and A Ponton, *A Green Manifesto* (McDonald Optima, London, 1988); J Button, *How to be Green* (Hutchinson, London, 1990); and D Wall, *Getting There: Steps to a Green Society* (Green Print, London, 1990).
10 Department of the Environment, *This Common Inheritance*, pp268-9. See also Department of the Environment, *Green Rights and Responsibilities: A Citizen's Guide to the Environment* (HMSO, London, 1992).

CONCLUSION

Having set out the central debates surrounding the politics of the environment, the conclusions focus on four outstanding issues.

CRITERIA FOR JUDGING ENVIRONMENTAL INITIATIVES

The concept of sustainable development has recurred throughout this book. It is the obvious benchmark against which policies should be judged to see if, and how far, they are environmentally friendly. Chapter 8 distinguished three different interpretations of sustainable development. The purist interpretation is that of the radical greens discussed in Chapter 9. There, a distinction was drawn between the dark green radical view and the weaker, reformist perspective. This light green interpretation of sustainable development links with the pragmatist version. The purist/pragmatist split parallels the Fundi/Realo debate within green parties. The third, tokenist, interpretation does not aim to take sustainable development seriously. It is concerned to carry on as before, with a few gestures to the environment.

These three perspectives provide criteria from which policies or documents can be judged. For example, when the government publishes, late in 1993, the Agenda 21 document it agreed to prepare at Rio, tokenists will say it is fine and purists will say it is worse than useless. Pragmatists will look for things in it about which they can make encouraging noises. It is necessary for environmentalists to work out where they stand on the arguments and the different interpretations. Only in this way can the individual develop criteria by which to judge environmental policies. Without clear criteria, discussion quickly becomes confused.

GREEN PROSPECTS IN BRITAIN

There are two main reasons why Britain's ability to come to terms with the range of environmental problems which faces it in the 1990s is limited. First, the machinery of central government is weak. Government has not adopted the principles of sustainable development in the day-to-day business of governing. Also conflict between the DTp and DoE over the range of environmental problems associated with a roads-based transport policy illustrates the lack of effective coordination. Policy contradictions are made worse by weak leadership. This is illustrated by confusion over a proposed Environmental Protection Agency. John Major proposed bringing the regulatory agencies discussed in Chapter 5 – HMIP, NRA and the WRAs – together into such an agency. This unleashed a bitter Whitehall dispute between MAFF and the DoE, and the proposed legislation was dropped.

Britain's second handicap is its voluntarist approach to tackling pollution problems.[1] In accepting pollution levels to air or water above normal requirements regulators have put business interests ahead of environmental concerns. Cynics argue that BATNEEC – the best available techniques not entailing excessive costs – has given way to CATNIP – cheapest available technology not involving prosecution. This approach is based on persuasion and compromise and is inherently weak. The ethos of HMIP, which acts against rigorous enforcement, has also been much criticised.[2]

The NRA, a new organisation establishing a new ethos, has taken a tougher approach. In its first three and a half years of life (up to April 1993), it dealt with about 115 000 reported incidents. Of these, 1776 were Category 1, major pollution incidents. The NRA secured prosecution in 548 of these cases. Fifty one further cases had yet to be resolved by the courts. Overall, the NRA wins about 95 per cent of the cases it brings. Although it has secured prosecution in only 2 per cent of all reported incidents, it has been successful about a third of all Category 1 cases.[3]

Attempts to strengthen the voluntarist approach are further undermined by the secrecy that surrounds it. Despite attempts to publish more information, negotiation of BATNEEC agreements continues to be undertaken in private. This parallels the way in which business interests still dominate policy making in such fields as road building and nuclear power, which have always proved inhospitable terrain for environmentalists. The decision early in 1993 not to proceed with registers of contaminated land is another example of secrecy placing commercial interests before environmental concerns. The role of the Citizen's Charter initiative in making government behave in more environmentally-sensitive ways has yet to be clarified.

It is not just in the industrial sphere that the traditional, voluntarist approach undermines the impact of policies on environmental problems. Chapter 6 outlined how the same approach limits government attempts to change individuals' behaviour.

In terms of the tokenist and pragmatist criteria discussed above, Britain's approach began the 1990s as tokenist and looks set to continue in that vein during the mid 1990s. But policy areas differ, as Chapters 2 and 5 showed. In wildlife, for example, some more seriously considered, pragmatist approaches are starting to emerge.

However, for radical greens applying purist criteria the 1990s look bleak. The Green Party has established a bridgehead of about 5 to 10 per cent in some countries but it has been marginalised in Britain. Any prospects for change will depend on a long-term push combining the four extra-parliamentary approaches discussed in Chapter 9. Bottom-up change via empowering approaches to participation exercises in connection with Local Agenda 21s, and via the development of TFOs, may lead to considerable improvements in some areas. Such moves can be promoted by local councils developing a strong political and administrative commitment to environmental change. Certainly, post-Rio, there is widespread appreciation of the enormous potential for local action. But, overall, the scope for radical moves towards purist interpretations is very limited. This raises the issue of how those who believe in purist approaches should react to government initiatives that fall into the tokenist and pragmatist categories.

THE MORAL HIGH GROUND

It is environmental groups that face the greatest dilemma here. Many are trying to promote purist interpretations of sustainable development. Yet they understand that politics is politics, and that government cannot leap from a strategy based on growth to purist interpretations of sustainable development in five minutes. However, if groups are to change Whitehall's approach, they have to communicate and get into a developing dialogue. To do that they have to compromise. But dialogue offers long-term opportunities to educate government and wean it off growth. The same dilemma faces local groups.

Purists say groups should stick to the moral high ground. They feel compromise undermines the coherence of the inter-related ideas of sustainable development. Not only do groups lose their credibility, they also convey a damaging message. By contrast, pragmatists argue that this approach leads nowhere, as government will not change unless attempts are made to persuade it to do so. For them dialogue is the only way forward. They see purists being left talking solely to people who agree with them, isolated in a cul de sac.

A practical example of whether to compromise or not sometimes confronts wildlife groups. Many disapprove of environmental economics and cost-benefit approaches. But there are circumstances in which going along with putting a value on a site can help to protect it or provide a replacement. You cannot reproduce an ancient water-meadow in a year or two, but ponds are habitats that *can* be recreated quite quickly. The cost of doing so can be calculated. Experiments are being conducted into creating new saltmarsh to replace what is lost to rising sea levels on the east coast. It is not yet known how widely applicable this replacement strategy may turn out to be.

The dilemma that faces groups also confronts individuals committed to radical ideas. Many greens who regularly bought Ecover products in the early 1990s were confused when Group 4 subsequently spent £4.5 million on a 50 per cent holding in the company. Chapter 2 recounted how Group 4 was the firm responsible for throwing protesters off Twyford Down. Nevertheless, many disagreed with the Green Party's decision to recommend a boycott of Ecover products.

THE ENVIRONMENT AND THE POLITICAL AGENDA

In July 1989, just after the Greens' 15 per cent vote in the European election, a MORI poll found that 35 per cent of respondents considered the environment to be among the most important issues facing the government. In mid 1993 that figure was 3 per cent. However, the environment is likely to stay on the political agenda. To begin with, there is the argument of Chapter 1. We face a serious set of inter-related problems and our current approach to development and growth cannot be sustained. This central truth jumps into the media when there are disasters or new scientific findings on issues like ozone depletion to report.

Secondly, there is an environmental lobby and international NGOs which are ready to maximise the impact of news stories. Next, there is the continuing presence of the voters highlighted in Chapter 3. These are the young, educated people interested in quality of life and environmental issues. It remains to be seen how far future first-time voters will adopt the ideas of the 'New Politics', thus encouraging post-materialist voting patterns.

Finally, the environment is likely to retain a hold on Whitehall's agenda because of international pressures. Even if it is low on the public agenda, ministers and civil servants will still have to respond to EC directives, and international treaty obligations. Further, they will need to prepare for and attend EC, UN and other meetings to discuss the unravelling post-Rio agenda. The analysis of Chapter 1 suggests that environmental problems will get worse with time.

However, the evidence of this book suggests that it will be at least a decade before British government manages to usher on board new pilots to turn its supertanker around, so that it can be steered towards the safer haven of sustainable development. Many hazards are yet to be negotiated. One of them is the *capacity* of the state to carry out policies effectively. This emerges strongly from a study of governmental responses to Rio.[4] During the 1990s it looks as if tackling environmental problems will increasingly depend on action at the local and international levels, and not at the level of the nation state.

NOTES

1 Carter *et al.*, op cit.
2 Rydin, op cit, pp.352-4.
3 National Rivers Authority, *Annual Report 1991-92* (NRA, Bristol, 1992) and *Annual Report 1992-93* (NRA, Bristol, 1993).
4 Thomas, op cit.

A BRIEF GUIDE TO FURTHER READING

The best introductory books for each aspect of environmental politics are given in the notes at the end of each chapter. I have deliberately chosen books with extensive lists of further references.

A stimulating and very readable account of green ideas is still J Porritt, *Seeing Green* (Blackwell, Oxford, 1984). For more challenging introductions see A Dobson, *Green Political Thought* (Unwin Hyman, London, 1990), R Goodin, *Green Political Theory* (Polity, Cambridge, 1992), or R Eckersley, *Environmentalism and Political Theory: Towards An Ecocentric Approach* (UCL Press, London, 1992).

For a deep ecology perspective see Bill Devall, *Simple in Means, Rich in Ends: Practising Deep Ecology* (Green Print, London, 1990).

On green economics contrast D Pearce *et al.*, *Blueprint For A Green Economy* (Earthscan, London, 1989) with P Ekins *et al.*, *Wealth Beyond Measure* (Gaia, London, 1992). M Jacobs, *The Green Economy* (Pluto, London, 1991), is complex: the essence of his ideas may be found in *Sustainable Development: Greening the Economy*, Fabian Tract 538 (Fabian Society, London, 1990).

On British environmental policy see the 1990 White Paper issued by the Department of the Environment, *This Common Inheritance: Britain's Environmental Strategy*, Cm 1200 (HMSO, London, 1990), or the 1991 annual report (Cm 1655), or the 1992 annual report (Cm 2068). *The UK Strategy For Sustainable Development* is due to be published late in 1993. For a critical discussion see J McCormick, *British Politics and the Environment* (Earthscan, London, 1991), or – more challenging – A Weale, *The New Politics of Pollution* (Manchester University Press, Manchester, 1992).

A forecasting approach is taken in D Meadows, D Meadows and J Randers, *Beyond the Limits* (Earthscan, London, 1992), which is an updated version of their 1971 book.

Commentary on events and new books can be found in such journals as *Town and Country Planning, Resurgence, The Ecologist, and*

New Economics. More academic are *Environmental Politics*, and *Environmental Values*.

If you are trying to track down an organisation you need the latest edition of *Who's Who in the Environment* (The Environment Council, London, annual). It is misleadingly titled: it lists hundreds of organisations involved with different aspects of the environment, and has a subject index and an organisation index.

If you are looking for ideas about how to run a group campaign, try M Wright (ed), *Our Backyard: How to Challenge the Threats to Your Health and Environment* (Hodder and Stoughton, London, 1991), or D Wilson, *Citizen Action: Taking Action in Your Community* (Longman, Harrow, 1986). Books such as these contain long lists of addresses and further publications. Anti-roads campaigners operate in special circumstances defined by different sets of rules from all other planning disputes: see W Sheate and M Sullivan, *Campaigners' Guide to Road Proposals* (CPRE, London, 1993).

If you want to green your life-style, try J Button, *How to be Green* (Hutchinson, London, 1990). If you are thinking of green work opportunities try H D'Arcy and G Sharp, *Your Green Career* (Roosters Ltd, London, 1991), or Institution of Environmental Sciences, *Environmental Careers Handbook* (Trotman and Company, Richmond, 1993).

If you fancy a green novel try E Abbey, *The Monkey Wrench Gang* (Robin Clark, London, 1991), first published in 1973, J Mortimer, *Titmus Regained* (Penguin, Harmondsworth, 1991), B Elton, *Gridlock* (Sphere, London, 1992), or J Giono, *The Man Who Planted Trees* (Peter Owen, London, 1989), first published in 1954.

INDEX

acid rain 7, 8, 56
Agalev 32-3
Agenda 21 28, 45-6, 51, 64, 80, 83,
103, 107, 109
Agricultural Development Advisory
Service 57
Agriculture Act 1986 49, 54, 62
Agriculture Act 1988 59, 62
Alarm UK 20
Alkali Act 1863 53, 54
Animal Liberation Front 22, 103
Antarctica 7, 43-4
Arctic 7

B&Q 73-4
BANANA 78
BATNEEC 60, 108
Bhopal disaster 7
biodiversity 8-9, 44
convention 44-5
bioregionalism 99-100
Body Shop 72
BPEO 60
British Housebuilders' Federation 20
British Rail 57
British Roads Federation 20
British Tourist Authority 57
British Trust for Conservation Volunteers
28
Brundtland Report 13, 14, 54, 56, 88
Bush, George 44, 78

California 10, 81-2
catalytic converters 85, 93
CATNIP 108
Centre for Alternative Technology 103
Chernobyl 7, 54
chlorofluorocarbons (CFCs) 8, 22, 43,
48, 64, 71, 74
civic trusts 20
Clean Air Act 1956 53, 54, 77
climate change convention 45, 46
Clinton, Bill 44, 78
Commons, Open Spaces and Footpaths
Preservation Society 17
Control of Pollution Act 1974 54
Council for the Preservation of Rural
England 18
Council for the Protection of Rural

England (CPRE) 17, 18, 20, 21, 23, 49
corporate social responsibility (CSR) 73
Country Landowners' Association 21
Countryside Commission (CC) 25, 57, 58
Countryside Council for Wales 58

Dafis, Cynog 38, 59
decentralisation 100
Department of Energy 58, 59
Department of the Environment (DoE)
49, 53, 56, 57, 58, 61, 108
Department of Trade and Industry (DTI)
57, 58, 59, 71
Department of Transport (DTp) 56, 59,
63-4, 108

Earth Centre 103-4
Earth First! 22
Earth Summit: see Rio Summit
Eco-Labelling Board 72
Ecolo 32-3
ecological modernisation 82, 88-90, 95
Ecover 72, 110
English Nature 58
environmental economics 96
environmental impact assessment (EIA)
25, 62
Environmental Protection Act 1990 (EPA)
49, 60-1, 67-8, 75, 78
Environmental Protection Agency (USA)
78
environmental refugees 10
Environmentally Sensitive Area (ESA)
62-3
ERM 51
European Commission 1-2, 20, 26, 47-8,
103
European Environment Agency 47
European Parliament 50
Exxon Valdese 7

Fison's 22
Forestry Commission 62
Forsyte, Soames 17
Foxley Wood, Hampshire 55
Friends of the Earth (FoE) 18, 21, 22, 40,
71-4
Fundi/Realo dispute 35, 103, 107

Garden Cities Association 18
Green 2000 38, 39
Green Consumer Guide, The 72
greenhouse effect 7, 8, 45
green parties 30-41
Green Party (UK) 36-40, 41, 56, 72, 74,
105, 109, 110

115